"Charge That to My Account"

and

Other Gospel Messages

BY

H. A. IRONSIDE, Litt. D.

CHICAGO

MOODY PRESS

Printed in the United States of America

PREFATORY NOTE

Because God has been pleased to set His seal of approval upon these simple gospel messages by using them in the awakening and salvation of sinners, they are now put out in book form in the earnest hope that many who read them may find joy and peace in believing.

H. A. IRONSIDE

CONTENTS

"Charge That to My Account"

CHAPTER I

"CHARGE THAT TO MY ACCOUNT"

"If thou count me therefore a partner, receive him as myself. If he hath wronged thee, or oweth thee ought, put that on mine account; I Paul have written it with mine own hand, I will repay it; albeit I do not say to thee how thou owest unto me even thine own self besides" (Philemon 17-19).

SOMEONE has said that this Epistle to Philemon is the finest specimen of early private Christian correspondence extant. We should expect this, since it was given by divine inspiration. And yet it all has to do with a thieving runaway slave named Onesimus, who was about to return to his former master.

The history behind the letter, which is deduced from a careful study of the Epistle itself, seems to be this: In the city of Colosse dwelt a wealthy Christian man by the name of Philemon, possibly the head of a large household, and like many in that day, he had a number of slaves or bondsmen. Christianity did not immediately overturn the evil custom of slavery, although eventually it was the means of practically driving it out of the whole civilized world. It began by regulating the relation of master and slave, thus bringing untold blessing to those in bondage.

This man Philemon evidently was converted through the ministry of the apostle Paul. Where they met, we are not told; certainly not in the city of Colosse, because in writing the letter to the Colossians, Paul makes it clear that he had never seen the faces of those who formed the Colossian church. You will recall that he labored at Ephesus for a long period. The fame of his preaching and teaching was spread abroad, and we read that "all in Asia heard the word." Among those who thus heard the Gospel message may have been this man Philemon of Colosse, and so he was brought to know Christ.

Some years had gone by, and this slave, Onesimus, had run away. Evidently before going, he had robbed his master. With his ill-gotten gains he had fled to Rome. How he reached there we do not know, but I have no doubt that upon his arrival he had his fling, and enjoyed to the full that which had belonged to his master. He did not take God into account, but nevertheless God's eye was upon him when he left his home, and it followed him along the journey from Colosse to Rome. When he reached that great metropolis, he was evidently brought into contact with the very man through whom his master, Philemon, had been converted. Possibly Onesimus was arrested because of some further rascality, and in that way came in contact with Paul in prison, or he may have visited him voluntarily. At any rate God, who knows just how to bring the needy sinner and the messenger of the Cross together, saw to it that Onesimus and Paul met face to face.

Sam Hadley Finds Jim

Some years ago there happened a wonderful illustration of this very thing: the divine ability to bring the needy sinner and the messenger of Christ together.

When Sam Hadley was in California, just shortly before he died, Dr. J. Wilbur Chapman, that princely man of God, arranged a midnight meeting, using the largest theatre in the city of Oakland, in order to get the message of Hadley before the very people who needed it most. On that night a great procession, maybe one thousand people, from all the different churches, led by the Salvation Army band, wended their way through the main streets of the city. Beginning at 10:30, they marched for one-half hour, and then came to the Metropolitan Theatre. In a moment or two it was packed from floor to gallery.

I happened to be sitting in the first balcony, looking right down upon the stage. I noticed that every seat on the stage was filled with Christian workers, but when Sam Hadley stepped forward to deliver the stirring message of the evening, his seat was left vacant. Just as he began to speak, I saw a man who had come in at the rear of the stage, slip around from behind the back curtain, and stand at one of the wings with his hand up to his ear, listening to the address. Evidently he did not hear very well. In a moment or two he moved to another wing, and then on to another one. Finally he came forward to one side of the front part of the stage and stood there listening, but still he could not hear very well. Upon noticing him, Dr. Chapman immediately got up, greeted the poor fellow, brought him to the front, and put him in the very chair which Sam Hadley had occupied. There he listened entranced to the story of Hadley's redemption.

When the speaker had finished, Dr. Chapman arose to close the meeting, and Hadley took Chapman's chair next to this man. Turning to the man he shook hands with him, and they chatted together. When Dr. Chapman was about ready to ask the people to rise and receive the benediction, Hadley suddenly sprang to his feet, and said, "Just a moment, my friends. Before we close, Dr. Chapman, may I say something? When I was on my way from New York to Oakland a couple of weeks ago, I stopped at Detroit. I was traveling in a private car, put at my disposal by a generous Christian manufacturer. While my car was in the yards, I went down town and addressed a group at a mission. As I finished, an old couple came up, and said, 'Mr. Hadley, won't you go home and take supper with us?'

"I replied, 'You must excuse me; I am not at all well, and it is a great strain for me to go out and visit between meetings. I had better go back to the car and rest.'

"They were so disappointed. The mother faltered. 'Oh, Mr. Hadley, we did want to see you so badly about something.'

"Very well, give me a few moments to lie down and I will go with you."

He then told how they sat together in the old-fashioned parlor, on the horse-hair furniture, and talked. They told him their story: "Mr. Hadley, you know we have a son, Jim. Our son was brought up to go to Sunday school and church, and oh, we had such hopes of him. But he had to work out rather early in life and he got into association with worldly men, and went down and down and down. By and by he came under the power of strong drink. We shall never forget the first time he came home drunk. Sometimes he would never get home at all until the early hours of the morning. Our hearts were breaking over him. One time he did not come all night, but early in the morning, after we had waited through a sleepless night for him, he came in hurriedly, with a pale face, and said, 'Folks, I cannot stay; I must get out. I did something when I was drunk last night, and if it is found out, it will go hard with me. I am not going to stay here and blot your name.' He kissed us both and left, and until recently we have never seen nor heard of him."

"Mr. Hadley, here is a letter that just came from a friend who lives in California, and he tells us, 'I am quite certain that I saw your son, Jim, in San Francisco. I was coming down on a street car, and saw him waiting for a car. I was carried by a block. I hurried back, but he had boarded another car and was gone. I know it was Jim.'

"He is still living, Mr. Hadley, and we are praying that God will save him yet. You are going to California to have meetings out there. Daily we will be kneeling here praying that God will send our boy, Jim, to hear you, and perhaps when he learns how God saved one poor drunkard, he will know there is hope also for him. Will you join us in daily prayer?"

"I said I would, and we prayed together. They made me promise that every day at a given hour, Detroit time, I would lift my heart to God in fellowship with them, knowing that they were kneeling in that room, praying God that He would reach Jim, and give me the opportunity of bringing him to Christ. That was two weeks ago. I have kept my promise every day. My friends, this is my first meeting in California, and here is Jim. Tonight he was drinking in a saloon on Broadway as the great procession passed. He heard the singing, followed us to the theatre, and said, 'I believe I will go in.' He hurried up here, but it was too late. Every place was filled, and the police officer said, 'We cannot allow another person to go inside.' Jim thought, 'This is just my luck. Even if I want to go and hear the gospel, I cannot. I will go back to the saloon.' He started back; then he returned determined to see if there was not some way to get in. He came in the back door, and finally sat in my own chair. Friends, Jim wants Christ, and I ask you all to pray for him."

There that night we saw that poor fellow drop on his knees, and confess his sin and guilt, and accept Christ as his Saviour. The last sight we had of Jim was when J. Wilbur Chapman and he were on their way to the Western Union Telegraph office to send the joyful message: "God heard your prayers. My soul is saved." Oh, what a God, lover of sinners that He is! How He delights to reach the lost and needy!

"He Delighteth in Mercy"

This same God was watching over Onesimus. He saw him when he stole that money, and as he fled from his master's house. He watched him on his way to Rome, and in due time brought him face to face with Paul. Through that same precious gospel that had been blest to the salvation of Philemon, Onesimus, the thieving runaway slave, was also saved, and another star was added to the Redeemer's crown.

Then I can imagine Onesimus coming to Paul, and saying, "Now, Paul, I want your advice. There is a matter which is troubling me. You know my master, Philemon. I must confess that I robbed him and ran away. I feel now that I must go back, and try to make things right."

One evidence that people are really born of God is their effort to make restitution for wrong done in the past. They want a good conscience both before God and man.

"Paul, ought I to go back in accordance with the Roman law? I have nothing to pay, and I don't know just what to do. I do not belong to myself, and it is quite impossible to ever earn anything to make up for the loss. Will you advise me what to do?"

Paul might have said, "I know Philemon well. He has a tender, kind, loving heart and a forgiving spirit. I will write him a note and ask him to forgive you, and that will make everything all right."

But he did not do that. Why? I think that he wanted to give us a wonderful picture of the great gospel of vicarious substitution. One of the primary aspects of the work of the Cross is substitution. The Lord Jesus Christ Himself paid the debt that we owe to the infinite God, in order that when forgiveness came to us it would be on a perfectly righteous basis. Paul, who had himself been justified through the Cross, now says, "I will write a letter to Philemon, and undertake to become your surety. You go back to Philemon, and present my letter. You do not need to plead your own case; just give him my letter."

We see Onesimus with that message from Paul safely hidden in his wallet, hurrying back to Colosse. Imagine Philemon standing on the portico of his beautiful residence, looking down the road, and suddenly exclaiming, "Why, who is that? It certainly looks like that scoundrel, Onesimus! But surely he would not have the face to come back. Still, it looks very much like him. I will just watch and wait.

A little later, he says, "I declare, it *is* Onesimus! He seems to be coming to the house. I suppose he has had a hard time in the world. The stolen money is all gone, and now perhaps he is coming to beg for pardon."

As he comes up the pathway, Onesimus calls, "Master, Master!"

"Well, Onesimus, are you home again?"

"Yes, Master, read this, please."

No other word would Onesimus speak for himself; Paul's letter would explain all.

Philemon takes the letter, opens it, and begins to read: *Paul, a prisoner of Jesus Christ.*

"Why Onesimus, where did you meet Paul? Did you see him personally?"

"Yes, Master, in the prison in Rome; he led me to Christ."

Unto Philemon our dearly beloved, and fellowlabourer.

"Little enough I have ever done, but that is just like Paul."

And to our beloved Apphia. (That was Mrs. Philemon.)

"Come here, Apphia. Here is a letter from Paul." When Mrs. Philemon sees Onesimus, she exclaims, "Are you back?"

One can imagine her mingled disgust and indignation as she sees him standing there. But Philemon says: "Yes, my dear, not a word. Here is a letter for us to read—a letter from Paul."

Running on down the letter he comes to this: *Yet for love's sake I rather beseech thee, being such an one as Paul the aged, and now also a prisoner of Jesus Christ. I beseech thee for my son Onesimus.*

"Think of that! He must have been putting it over on Paul in some way or another."

Whom I have begotten in my bonds. "I wonder if he told him anything about the money he stole from us. I suppose he has been playing the religious game with Paul."

Which in time past was to thee unprofitable.

"I should say he was."

But now profitable to thee and to me.

"I am not so sure of that."

Whom I have sent again.

"Paul must have thought a lot of him. If he didn't serve him any better than he did me, he would not get much out of him." He goes on reading through the letter.

"Well, well, that rascally, thieving liar! Maybe Paul believes that he is saved, but I will never believe it unless I find out that he owned up to the wrong he did me."

What is this? *If he hath wronged thee, or oweth thee ought, put that on my account; I Paul have written it with mine own hand, I will repay it: albeit I do not say to thee how thou owest unto me even thine own self besides.*

Oh, I think in a moment Philemon was conquered. "Why," he says, "it is all out then. He has confessed his sin. He has acknowledged his thieving, owned his guilt, and, just think, Paul, that dear servant of God, suffering in prison for Christ's sake, says: *Put that on my account. I will settle everything for him.* Paul becomes his surety." It was just as though Paul should write today: "Charge that to my account!"

A Gospel Picture

Is not this a picture of the gospel? A picture of what the Saviour has done for every repentant soul? I think I see

Him as he brings the needy, penitent sinner into the presence of God, and says, "My Father, he has wronged Thee, he owes Thee much, but all has been charged to My account. Let him go free." How could the Father turn aside the prayer of His Son after that death of shame and sorrow on Calvary's cross, when He took our blame upon Himself and suffered in our stead?

But now observe it is not only that Paul offered to become Onesimus' surety, it was not merely that he offered to settle everything for Onesimus in regard to the past, but he provided for his future too. He says to Philemon: *"If thou count me therefore a partner, receive him as myself."*

Is not that another aspect of our salvation? We are "accepted in the beloved." The blessed Saviour brings the redeemed one into the presence of the Father, and says, "My Father, if thou countest Me the partner of Thy throne, receive him as Myself." Paul says, *"Not now as a servant, but above a servant, a brother beloved, specially to me, but how much more unto thee, both in the flesh, and in the Lord?"* He is to take the place, not of a bondsman, but of an honored member of the family and a brother in Christ. Think of it —once a poor, thieving, runaway slave, and now a recognized servant of Christ, made welcome for Paul's sake. Thus our Father saves the lawless, guilty sinner, and makes him welcome for Jesus' sake, treating him as He treats His own beloved Son.

> "Jesus paid it all,
>   All to Him I owe;
> Sin had left a crimson stain:
>   He washed it white as snow."

And now every redeemed one is "in Christ before God— yea, made the righteousness of God in him." Oh, wondrous love! Justice is satisfied. What a picture we have here then of substitution and acceptance. The apostle Paul epitomized it all for us: "Who was delivered for our offences, and was raised again for our justification" (Romans 4:25).

We are accepted in the Beloved. The Lord Jesus became our Surety, settled for all our past, and has provided for all our future. In the book of Proverbs (11:15), there is a very striking statement, "He that is surety for a stranger shall smart for it; and he that hateth suretiship is sure." These words were written centuries before the Cross, to warn men of what is still a very common ground for failure and ruin in business life. To go surety for a stranger is a very danger- ous thing, as thousands have learned to their sorrow. It is poor policy to take such a risk unless you are prepared to lose.

But there was One who knew to the full what all the con- sequences of His act would be, and yet, in grace, deigned to become "Surety for a stranger." Meditate upon these won- derful words: "For ye know the grace of our Lord Jesus Christ, that, though he was rich, yet for your sakes he be- came poor, that ye through his poverty might be rich" (2 Corinthians 8:9). He was the stranger's Surety.

A surety is one who stands good for another. Many a man will do this for a friend, long known and trusted; but no wise man will so act for a stranger, unless he is prepared to lose. But it was when we were strangers and foreigners and ene- mies, and alienated in our minds by wicked works, that Jesus in grace became our Surety. "Christ also hath once suffered for sins, the just for the unjust, that he might bring us to God."

All we owed was exacted from Him when He suffered upon the tree for sins, not His own. He could then say, "I restored that which I took not away" (Psalm 69:4). Bishop Lowth's beautiful rendering of Isaiah 53:7 reads: "It was exacted and He became answerable." This is the very es- sence of the Gospel message. He died in my place; He paid my debt.

How fully He proved the truth of the words quoted from Proverbs, when He suffered on that cross of shame! How He had to "smart for it" when God's awful judgment against sin fell upon Him. But He wavered not! In love to God and to the strangers whose Surety He had become, "He endured the cross, despising the shame."

His sorrows are now forever past. He has paid the debt, met every claim in perfect righteousness. The believing sinner is cleared of every charge, and God is fully glorified.

> "He bore on the tree
>   The sentence for me,
> And now both the Surety
>   And sinner are free."

None other could have met the claims of God's holiness against the sinner and have come out triumphant at last. He alone could atone for sin. Because He has settled every claim, God has raised Him from the dead, and seated Him at His own right hand in highest glory.

Have you trusted "the stranger's Surety"? If not, turn to Him now while grace is free.

CHAPTER II

THE WAY TO THE CITY

"The labour of the foolish wearieth every one of them, because he knoweth not how to go to the city" (Ecclesiastes 10:15).

IN some respects the book of Ecclesiastes is the saddest in all the Bible. It gives the search of the natural man for the supreme good under the sun, leading at last only to bitter disappointment and the heart-broken cry: "Vanity of vanities; all is vanity . . . all is vanity and vexation of spirit" (Eccl. 1:2, 14).

There is a city presented to the eye of faith in the blessed Bible for which every Christian heart yearns, a city toward which the saints of God in all ages have turned their eyes. We are told that Abraham, the father of the faithful, looked for that city "which hath foundations, whose builder and maker is God" (Hebrews 11:10). So dear was it to him that he went forth not knowing whither he went, and turned his back on all worldly prospects, that he might be sure of a place in that city.

In the New Testament, our blessed Lord tells us: "In my Father's house are many mansions: if it were not so, I would have told you" (John 14:2), and then He adds, "I go to prepare a place for you." In that last wonderful book of the Bible, the book of the Revelation, the description of that city is beyond anything that these poor finite minds of ours can comprehend. It is a city with a street of gold, with foundations of precious stones, with gates of pearl, and walls of diamonds; for the jasper of the book of Revelation is clear as crystal, and not the opaque jasper that we know, but evidently the diamond in all its glory. In this way we are given to understand something of what God has provided for those who love Him. What a solemn thing to miss the way to that city! We dwell in this world for some fifty, sixty, seventy, or even eighty years, and if, after we have passed our little life here, we find ourselves going out into a dark eternity, what a tragedy life will really be!

In this book, Solomon uses a very striking figure. He imagines a countryman on his way to the city, desiring to go perhaps to the great capital of Palestine—Jerusalem, or to some other city upon which his heart is set. But that man starts out trying to find his way with neither guide-post to direct him, nor authoritative information to tell him which route to take. He tries first one road and then another, only to be disappointed every time, until at last, utterly wearied, he throws himself down in despair as the shades of night are falling, and says, "It is no use, I cannot make it; I cannot find my way." "The labour of the foolish wearieth every one of them, because he knoweth not how to go to the city."

If we think of that city as heaven, or as the glorious New Jerusalem, then indeed we may see how aptly Solomon's words apply to myriads of mankind about us. Speak to men about their hope of heaven and they will say uncertainly, "Oh, yes, I trust I shall enter heaven when earth's short day is over; I hope I shall find my way to the city of God; I hope that some day my feet will walk the gold-paved street of the New Jerusalem." If you ask them what assurance they have that they are really on the road that leads to heaven, you will find that they are all in confusion. Many of them will not even thank you for trying to give them authoritative information from the Word of God. Instead of "Thus saith the Lord," you will find them substituting, "I think." What a common thing it is to hear men say, "I think that everything will come out all right in the end; there are many different roads to eternity, many men of many minds, but we are all going to the same place at last; every road will eventually lead to heaven, we hope." But you know that this is not logical, it is not reasonable. It is a principle that does not work in this life, nor in this world, and what reason have we to believe that it will work when we come to another life, and another world?

The Wrong Train

I remember one day leaving Los Angeles by train to go to San Diego. Shortly after we passed Fullerton, my attention was directed to an altercation going on near me. I had observed a little old lady who got on at a station some miles back. My attention was drawn to her because of the great number of bundles she carried. In one hand she had a cage, evidently containing a parrot, some kind of package held by one finger, a grip, and a bag; but she got in and put them all down about her, and filled the entire space where she sat. She was nicely settled when the conductor came around, and said, "Tickets, please." She handed him her ticket, and he said, "Madam, this is not your train. Your ticket calls for San Bernardino, and you are on the train that goes to San Diego."

"You needn't tell me that," she replied; "I asked a man before I got on, and he told me that this train was going to San Bernardino."

"Well," he said, "I am sorry, but you have been the victim of some wrong information, for this train is going to San Diego."

"I don't believe it," she said; "I bought this ticket in good faith, and have taken the train they told me to take."

"Pardon me," he replied, "but I am the conductor on this train, and it is going to San Diego. If you want to go to

San Bernardino, you will have to get off and take a train back."

Finally as the train drew near to the next stop, she gathered up her parrot and her packages and bags, declaring that this was an outrage, and that she would report it to the company and have the conductor discharged for putting her off the train. She left, while the rest of the passengers smiled even though they felt sorry for her.

It is not true that if you take a train going north, you will land somewhere in the south. It is not true that if you are on the road leading to everlasting judgment, you will reach heaven. "The labour of the foolish wearieth every one of them, because he knoweth not how to go to the city."

Well Marked Roads

How grateful are those who have done much motoring for the wonderful way in which the various automobile associations, and also the state and federal governments, have marked the roads all over this great country. We start off in our cars, and every little while we see the signs directing us. When we come to a fork in the road, we are careful to take the right one. But sometimes you get into a region where the roads have not been marked, and how perplexing it often is.

I remember of the time we were going from Elizabeth, New Jersey, to California. We were away out in Arizona, and came to a fork in the road. There had been a sign there, but some young vandals had evidently used it as a mark for shooting, and had shot it up so completely that we could not make anything out of it. My secretary, the young man who was driving, said, "I think this is the right road," but I said, "No, I think this is the one." Our thoughts did not amount to anything. We went wrong and got far out of our route, and had to retrace our way many long miles. The labor of the foolish wearied us. Why? Because we did not know the way to the city, we had no authoritative information. How many eternity-bound men and women are content to go on just like that! What egregious folly when God's Word has so plainly marked out the only right way!

Several Wrong Roads

May I indicate some of the roads which men and women take, and which they think will lead them to heaven?

First, there is *Legality Lane*. Do you know that lane? It is a hard, stone road, and many imagine that it will get them through to heaven. As you pass along you see the frowning cliffs of Mt. Sinai, you hear the heavy thunderings and see the lightning flashing, and you can almost hear the words: "Cursed is every one that continueth not in all things which are written in the book of the law to do them."

But you say, "I will do my best; I will try to keep God's holy commands; I will surely get to heaven at last." Beware, for *Legality Lane* will bring you eventually to the place of the curse, for God's Word declares that if a man shall "keep the whole law and yet offend in one point, he is guilty of all" (James 2:10). Again we read, "And cursed is everyone that continueth not in all things which are written in the book of the law to do them" (Galatians 3:10). No man was ever justified by the works of the law, and no man ever will be. It is utterly impossible that man should wash out the stains of sin by obedience to that holy law. The law tells you how to behave, but it does not tell you what to do if you have already failed and become guilty before God. *Legality Lane* will never lead you to the New Jerusalem.

Then says some one, "I will try *Reformation Alley*. It is true I have failed, I have been guilty of many gross violations of God's law; I have sinned, but I will turn over a new leaf, begin henceforth to please God, put away my bad habits, cultivate good ones, and surely all this will bring me at length to heaven." But my friend, this road will lead you eventually to eternal disappointment too, for there is a solemn word found in this same Book that reads like this, "God requireth that which is past" (Eccl. 3:15). Even though you were to reform today, even though you were to turn over a new leaf and never have another black mark upon the books, the old leaves with all their sinful record are still there, and you will have to face them in the day of judgment, unless some means shall be found whereby those marks can be blotted out.

"God requireth that which is past." Your grocer does that, you know, and it is perfectly right that he should. You run up a bill for a month or two, and then say, "Dear me, this will never do; this buying on credit is too easy a way to get head over heels in debt. I am going to begin to pay cash for everything I buy." And so you go down to the grocer with your market basket, and say, "I am determined to turn over a new leaf."

"In what regard?" the grocer asks.

"I have concluded that this buying on credit is all a mistake, and henceforth I am going to pay cash."

"I am delighted to hear that," he replies, "and when will you be able to settle your old bill?"

"Oh," you say, "you don't understand. I am going to pay cash from now on. Surely you won't hold the old account against me."

"I cannot afford to do business that way," he replies; "you received the groceries from me, and I will expect you to pay for them."

"But if I tell you that I am sorry, and pay you as I buy in the future, surely that ought to satisfy you." But he answers, "I will be delighted to have you as a cash customer, but business makes it necessary that I should require that which is past."

My friend, you may reform, you may turn over a new leaf, but when you get to the end of *Reformation Alley,* you will find that you have landed in a district called Eternal Disappointment, where you hear the sad voice of the Son of God saying: "Depart from me, I never knew you."

There is another highway that runs very close along side this one, it is called *Morality Road.* Many excellent people travel along this way. People whom you would be glad to have in your home, travel this road. You would find pleasure in their society. They are people who eschew all kinds of evil behavior, and pride themselves upon their morals and their ethics. They are what the world calls "good people," but they have no place in their thinking for the Lord Jesus Christ; and yet the Word of God declares: "There is none other name under heaven given among men, whereby we must be saved," but the name of Jesus. My friend, if morals could have saved, if ethics could have fitted you for heaven, Jesus Christ would never have died on Calvary's cross. Down in Gethsemane's garden He cried in the agony of His soul, "O my Father, if it be possible, let this cup pass from me," and if there had been any other way of saving sinners than through His sacrificial death, it would then have been made known.

Right by the side of Morality Road runs *Self-righteousness Boulevard.* It is a magnificent boulevard indeed, and here the scribes and Pharisees and many church dignitaries walk. Listen to one of them crooning his own perfections, as he cries, "I thank God I am not as other men. I am not a drunkard, I am not a blasphemer, I am not an adulterer; I fast twice in the week, I give tithes of all that I possess. Surely if any one gets to heaven I will." But hear the solemn declaration of the Word of God, "All our righteousnesses are as filthy rags." And that expression, *filthy rags,* does not mean shreds of clothing that have been contaminated by the dirt of the streets, but it refers to robes tainted and made unclean through the inward corruption that has exuded from the sores of lepers. Naaman, the leper, wearing his magnificent robes might throw off one of these garments, and say, "Look, I want to make you a gift, take this." Would you thank him for the gift? No, you would say, "Keep it away from me, it is contaminated by the leprosy from within." That is what our own righteousnesses are like. They all come from a corrupt, evil heart, and therefore, they can never justify a guilty sinner before God. The end of *Self-righteousness Boulevard* is the lake of fire.

And then akin to this is another road that we will call *Ritualistic Avenue*. Did you ever meet any one on that road? I said to a young lady one day, "I am glad to see you in the meeting; are you a Christian?"

"Yes," she said, "I have been a member of such and such a church ever since I was a child."

"Pardon me," I said, "but you did not understand my question. Have you ever been born again?"

"I was baptized when I was only eight days old," she replied.

"You don't understand me yet," I said, "were you ever converted?"

"Oh yes," she said, "I was confirmed when I was twelve years of age, and took the sacrament for the first time, and I have been very careful to attend services and take the sacrament ever since. You can be sure I am all right."

She was flitting down *Ritualistic Avenue* imagining it was the road to heaven when it was really leading her as fast as time could carry her to the pit of the abyss, and if not saved, she would plunge over the cliff of time into the darkness of eternity only to find out that baptism cannot save, sacraments cannot save, church-joining cannot save. It is Jesus only that washes away sin and fits us for glory.

Then there is another popular road that many take today. It is called *Delusion Road*. The people on this road are those who will not have the simple gospel of this Book, they will not take the plain statements of the Bible as to the deity of our Lord Jesus Christ, as to His sacrificial atoning death on the cross, but are ready to listen to every kind of folly. As they go down that road you hear them muttering to themselves, "God is all and all is God." "God is good and good is God." "There is no such thing as evil and sin and death." "Every day, in every way, I am growing better and better."

Men are deluding themselves, shutting their eyes to the realities of life. Aristotle, the great Greek philosopher, was wiser than they, for he said, "If any man rejects the testimony of the five senses, there is nothing else on which to build." What can you do for a man who is suffering from the twinges of rheumatism, but who looks at you, and says, "There is no such thing as pain, no such thing as suffering." Or, a man who can be a victim of all kinds of sinful habits, and yet looks you in the eye, and says, "There is no such thing as sin." Or, a man who can stand by the body of a dead loved one, and say, "There is no such thing as death"?

Scripture affirms, "Woe unto them that call evil good, and good evil; that put darkness for light, and light for darkness; that put bitter for sweet, and sweet for bitter" (Isaiah 5:20). *Delusion Road* will end at last in an eternal hell, and men will wake up too late to find out that sin is a reality, that death is a reality, that heaven is a reality and they have missed it, that hell is a reality and it is to be their place of abode forever. What a fearful thing it is to turn from God and trust in fables, to turn away from the sign-post that God has given to point the way to the city of God and take the opposite direction, hoping to reach heaven at last. "If therefore the light that is in thee be darkness, how great is that darkness!" (Matthew 6:23).

The Modernism Way

Another road is called *Modern Thought Highway*. Many of the intelligencia tread that path. It is dotted with universities and schools of higher education, and we find people peddling books up and down this highway, for the folk on this road are the learned of this world. They are too proud to accept, "Thus saith the Lord," but bow down before science, before modern thought, before philosophy, and all he differen delusions that are turning men away from God. Let me ead you the testimony of a man who admits that he is treading this road. It is written by Professor Melinowski:

> "Personally, I am an agnostic. That is, I am not able to deny the existence of God: nor would I be inclined to do so, still less to maintain that such a belief is not necessary. I also fervently hope that there is a survival after death, and I deeply desire to obtain some certainty on this matter. But with all that, I am unable to accept any positive religion—Christian or otherwise. I cannot positively believe in Providence in any sense of the word, and I have no conviction of personal immortality."

In other words, this man says, "I should like to go to the city of God, if there be such a city. I should like to spend my eternity there. But I cannot trust the Guide Book, I cannot believe the sign-post, I cannot put my confidence in One who says He came from there and went back, and is Himself the Way there." Yet this man is a great deal more modest than many who tread this road. He goes on to say:

> "Thus, as you see, I profoundly differ from the confident rationalist or disbeliever of the past generation or two. We all know the story of La Place and the discussion which he had with Napoleon the First about his system of Celestial Mechanics. The Emperor asked him: 'What place have you given to God in your system?' 'Sire,' was the answer, 'this is an hypothesis of which

I have never felt the need.' It is the proud answer of a
confident atheist, but it does not ring true to the humble
agnostic."

Men today will tell you frankly, "I never felt the need of
God; I do not need Him now, and I do not feel there will
be need for Him in eternity." But Melinowski continues:

"On the contrary, I should say that God is a reality and
not a hypothesis, and a reality of which I am in the greatest need, though this need I cannot satisfy or fulfill.
The typical rationalist says: 'I don't know, and I don't
care.' The tragic agostic would rejoin: 'I cannot
know, but I feel a deep and passionate need of faith, of
evidence, and of revelation.' Personally, to me, and to
those many who are like me, nothing really matters except the answer to the burning questions: 'Am I going
to live, or shall I vanish like a bubble? What is the aim,
and the sense, and the issue of all this strife and suffering?' The doubt of these two questions lives in us, and af-
fect all our thoughts and feelings. Modern agnosticism is
a tragic and shattering frame of mind. To dismiss agnosticism as an easy and shallow escape from the moral
obligations and discipline of religion—this is an unworthy
and superficial way of dealing with it. Is science responsible for my agnosticism and for that of others who
think like me? I believe it is, and therefore I do not love
science, though I have to remain its loyal servant. Is
there any hope of bridging this deepest gulf between
tragic agnosticism and belief? I do not know. Is there
any remedy? I cannot answer this either."

The blessed, holy Word of God answers every one of these
questions, but the modern mind turns away from it all, and
says, "No, I would rather go on questioning, go on in un-
certainty, than to face the problem of Jesus Christ."

But Jesus Christ is not a problem, He is the *solution* to
every problem for life, for death, and for eternity. Listen
to the poor woman at the well. Wonderingly she gazes at
the Jewish stranger who seems so ready to deal graciously

with the Samaritan, and she says, "I know that Messias cometh, which is called Christ: when he is come, he will tell us all things." Oh, the questions that were welling up in that woman's heart—"If I could only see Him maybe He would answer all my questions, maybe He would solve all my problems," and quietly, earnestly, kindly, Jesus looks upon her, and says, "I that speak unto thee am he." She took one long look into those fathomless eyes of His, and in a moment every question was answered, and back to the city she ran, and said to the men, "Come, see a man, which told me all things that ever I did: is not this the Christ?" Yes, He is the answer to every problem.

You remember it is written in Proverbs 14:12, "There is a way which seemeth right unto a man, but the end thereof are the ways of death." All these different pathways which have been indicated are the ways that seem right to man, but end in outer darkness. When Thomas asked the question, "Lord, how can we know the way?" Jesus answered, "I am the way, the truth, and the life: no man cometh unto the Father, but by me" (John 14:6).

Do you want to know the way to the city? Jesus is the Way. Do you want to know the truth in regard to the great problems of time and eternity? Jesus is the Truth. Do you want to know where life is found, so that you may be a new creature? Jesus is the Life. And, "He that believeth on the Son hath everlasting life: and he that believeth not the Son shall not see life; but the wrath of God abideth on him" (John 3:36). My friend, surely you want to find the way to the City. When at last you lie down and say good-by to your friends and loved ones, surely you want to be able to say, as one dear saint of God did, "Earth is receding and heaven is opening." If you do, you need Christ, for He alone is the Way to the city of God, and He says, "Him that cometh to me I will in no wise cast out" (John 6:37).

Are you saying, "I should like to find the way, I should like to know Christ, but how may I make His acquaintance?"

> "If I ask Him to receive me,
>   Will He say me nay?
> Not 'till earth and not 'till heaven,
>   Pass away."

If you will come as a sinner, confessing your guilt, forsaking every other refuge, and put your trust in Him alone, He will save you according to His Word, and you shall know Him as the only Way that leads to

> "Jerusalem, the golden,
> With milk and honey blest."

CHAPTER III

WILL A LOVING GOD PERMIT ANY ONE TO BE ETERNALLY LOST?

"He that believeth on the Son hath everlasting life: and he that believeth not the Son shall not see life; but the wrath of God abideth on him" (John 3:36).

OUR theme is in the form of a question, and the only place that we can find an answer to that question is in the Word of God. These poor minds of ours are utterly helpless in answering such a question. Men may reason as they will, but their reasonings will not change facts.

Apart from the revelation that God has given in His Word, we know nothing about what He will do in the eternal ages. One man may come to one conclusion, and another may come to a different one. We may say, "I think," or "I do not think," but our thinking will not alter the facts of the case. It is in the Word of God alone that this question is answered. Even if we fall back on mere human reason, it seems to me that no thinking person could come to the conclusion that a man could live in sin and die in sin, without suffering for his sins. "Be sure your sin will find you out" is an unalterable law of nature and of God.

Any argument that might be brought against a loving God permitting men and women to suffer throughout eternity because of sin, could also be brought against a loving God permitting men and women to suffer in this life because of sin. Joseph Cook, that stalwart New England fundamentalist, who lived before the word *"fundamentalist"* was coined, said something like this: One might imagine two angels talking together before the creation of the world, when they learned the divine secret that God was shortly to bring a universe into existence, and saying to each other:

"You have heard that God is going to create a world?"

"Yes."

"That He is going to have moral and intellectual beings in that world?"

"Yes."

"Not purely spiritual beings like ourselves, but beings with material bodies, and yet with minds and wills even as we angels have minds and wills of our own?"

"Yes, I have heard that such is His purpose. But can you answer this question? Do you think that our God will ever permit unhappiness to come into that world that He is going to create?"

"Oh, He certainly will not. Our kind, loving God will never permit unhappiness to come into the world that He is about to create."

"Do you think He will ever allow any of those creatures that He is going to bring into existence to act contrary to His holy will? Do you think He will ever permit sin to lift up its unholy head in the universe He is about to create?"

"Certainly not! Our God, our loving God, our holy God will never permit unholiness. He will never permit unrighteousness or wickedness to spoil that world that he is going to create."

"Do you think that God will ever allow man to suffer in pain and anguish in that world?"

"Oh, no! The world that God is going to create must of necessity be forever the abode of happy beings."

Can't you imagine angels reasoning something like that? But what are the facts? Six thousand years of human history, according to the chronology of the Hebrews, prove that a loving God did permit sin to come into the world, did permit wickedness to enter into this fair creation, and did permit pain, suffering, sorrow, broken hearts, unspeakable anguish, and even death to mar His fair creation.

The Reasonings of Men

Now just as holy beings might have reasoned before the creation of the world that God, because He is loving, because He is good, and because He is holy, would never permit sin to spoil this world, and would never permit suffering and sorrow and anguish to come in, so men reason today that a good God will not allow the effects of sin to go on for eternity. But how can you and I tell what God will permit unless He is pleased to reveal Himself in His own Word?

People say today, for example, reasoning from man up to God, "You are a father; would you ever put one of your children in a place of intense suffering, if you could help it? Would you ever willingly expose a child of yours to a fiery flame?"

Of course I answer, "No."

Then they ask, and they think they have good ground for what they are about to say, "If you as an earthly father would not allow a child of yours to suffer in this way, can you believe that a loving God will cast people into everlasting fire because of their sins?"

And I have to answer, "The only way I have of knowing what God will do is by observing what He has done, and by turning to the Word to see what He has to say."

He has permitted men and women and even little children, during the ages of time, to suffer unspeakable anguish. He has permitted innocent little children to be born into the world, the victims of incurable diseases handed down from their parents, and these diseases are often the result of the sins of their forebears. Many of these little children come into the world and grow up never knowing a moment without suffering and pain. Would you have expected that of God, from your idea of who God is and what He should do? Yet here are the facts, and we have to face them.

The only way we can account for these facts is that God hates sin, and in order to make men realize what a fearful thing it is to sin against Him, He allows dreadful consequences to befall those who commit sin, consequences affecting not only the one who commits the sin, but affecting generations yet to be born.

Men object to the statement in the law, "For I the Lord thy God am a jealous God, visiting the iniquity of the fathers upon the children unto the third and fourth generations of them that hate me" (Deuteronomy 5:9). And yet the facts prove that the Word of God is right, for He does this very thing. Sin must be a fearful affront to a holy God, or He would never have allowed the awful sufferings and horrors that have darkened the history of mankind. He wants us to understand that sin is the vilest, the blackest, the most dreadful thing in the universe. His Word says, "Be not deceived; God is not mocked; for whatsoever a man soweth, that shall he also reap" (Galatians 6:7).

Right in this world some men's sins are open, going before them to judgment. Some men suffer unspeakably during this life because of their sins, but, on the other hand, there are other men of whom this is not true. There are others who sin just as grievously, and yet there is no evidence that their sin is followed with anything like proper judgment in this world. There are men who live in luxury and pleasure upon the earth, utterly indifferent to the conditions of those around them, living selfishly for themselves alone, and indulging in all kinds of sins. Yet as far as this life is concerned, the punishment does not fall upon them, but if they are not reaping the due punishment in this life, depend upon it that in another world there will be a straightening up of the account, for it is written, "whatsoever a man soweth that shall he also reap." "Some men's sins are open, going before them into judgment, and some men they follow after." What does this sentence mean if God did not intend us to under- stand that men are not through with Him when they leave this world inpenitent? Some men's sins follow after them, and like the blood-hounds of hell which they are, they will track men down and drag them to the judgment bar of God where they shall give account of all the deeds done in the flesh.

The Time Element Involved

But some say, "What sin can a man commit during his brief years on earth to deserve eternal judgment?" Have you ever stopped to consider that a man can commit a hein- ous crime in a very short time for which we think he de- serves to be punished for all the rest of his natural life? Not very long ago a man of over seventy years of age came out of a prison in New England. Fifty years before he had been sentenced to that penitentiary for the horrible crime of murder. Because of his youth the law did not want to con- demn him to be hung, so he was sentenced to prison. Because of his desire for gain, he was stirred to anger, and in a mo- ment murdered a man, and no doubt he had many a month and year in which to repent of that crime. Yet society felt that it was only right that he should be shut away for fifty years. You see there may be no connection between the amount of time in which a man can commit a crime and the punishment that befits it.

Down in Kentucky there lived one of those fine southern gentlemen who had been left a widower. His wife, as she slipped away, left a darling baby who became all in all to him. He watched that child grow till she was a beautiful girl, and then on to budding young womanhood. By and by she returned from college, and was the very idol of his heart, and the apple of his eye. Then there came into that home a man who won the affection of that young woman and basely deceived her, luring her into grievous sin, ruined her sweet young life, and then cast her off, a poor broken-hearted girl. That father had been what is called a Universalist, but when that poor girl came sobbing, broken-hearted, seeking her father's house after weeks of wandering, during which she had been afraid to go home, and told him what had happened, and when he saw the wreck that had been made of the idol of his heart and life, he exclaimed, with an oath, "If God Almighty hasn't a hell for fiends like the one who has wrecked my happiness and ruined my child, He ought to make one!" And this Book says He has one, and it declares that "whoremongers, and sorcerers, and idolaters, and all liars" shall have their part in it for all eternity.

Why is eternal punishment the result of impenitent sin? Our Lord Jesus has told us in Mark's Gospel. What He actually said is obscured a little in our translation, but the Revised Version makes it clear. In Mark 3:28, we read, "Verily I say unto you, All sins shall be forgiven unto the sons of men, and blasphemies wherewith soever they shall blaspheme: but he that shall blaspheme against the Holy Ghost hath never forgiveness, but is in danger of eternal damnation." The Revised Version brings that out much more clearly: "Whosoever shall blaspheme against the Holy Spirit hath never forgiveness, but is guilty of an eternal sin." There you have it, the man who dies rejecting the Holy Spirit's testimony as to the Lord Jesus Christ is guilty of an eternal sin. That is why Scripture holds out no hope for his salvation in another world. The man who refuses the testimony the Holy Ghost has given concerning the Saviour's love, His marvelous atonement, and His wondrous grace has no other hiding place by which he may escape the wrath of a sin-hating God. And so I come back to the text with which I began, "He that believeth on the Son hath everlasting life: and he that believeth not the Son shall not see life; but the wrath of God abideth on him."

People say, "Oh, Paul or John or Peter may have believed this doctrine of eternal judgment for sin, but give me the words of Jesus—Jesus, the loving, gentle, tender, gracious, Galilean teacher—let me hear what Jesus says; His Word will be enough for me." Listen, my dear friends, no one ever spoke as seriously and as solemnly of the eternal consequences of sin as Jesus did. It is He who said, "If thine eye offend thee, pluck it out, and cast it from thee: it is better for thee to enter into life with one eye, rather than having two eyes to be cast into hell fire" (Matthew 18:9). It is Jesus who speaks so solemnly over and over again of that awful pit of woe, "Where their worm dieth not, and the fire is not quenched" (Mark 9:48). It is Jesus who said of Judas, "It had been good for that man if he had not been born," but if there is any possibility of Judas ever being saved, even after the lapse of countless ages of misery, I submit that it would be good for him that he had been born. But Jesus said, "Good for that man if he had not been born." That man sold his Saviour! Suppose you do the same thing? That man companied with Jesus for three and one-half years, and yet sinned against the Holy Ghost in rejecting Christ. You have heard the gospel over and over again, and if you should reject Him too, could it not be said of you: "Good for that man if he had not been born"?

But now it is Jesus again who utters these words, "He that believeth on the Son hath everlasting life." You cannot find fault with the love of God, for it gave Christ, and thereby provided a way of salvation. God is not holding you responsible because you are a sinner; you were born a sinner. You are not responsible because you have a sinful nature; you cannot help that. God is not going to cast you

away from His presence simply because that corrupt nature
has manifested itself in sin, for Christ has put away sin, and
any man who will may be saved from his sin through the
atoning work of the Lord Jesus Christ, and receive a new
nature. Why are men lost? The answer is clear: "He that
believeth not the Son shall not see life; but the wrath of
God abideth on him." You observe how this one sentence
plucks up by the very roots two modern forms of error in
regard to mankind.

There is Universalism. Is there any hope for a man who
dies rejecting Christ in this life, being saved in the life to
come? *"He that believeth not the Son shall not see life;
but the wrath of God abideth on him."* Jesus Himself could
not have put it more plainly than that. In this world God
is pleading with sinners, He is offering them salvation, but
if men reject His Son, it is the solemn declaration of Holy
Writ, they *shall not see life.* There is no hope in another
world for men who reject Christ in this.

But may it not be that the punishment for sin is nothing
more than utter annihilation? "He that believeth not the Son
shall not see life; but the wrath of God *abideth* on him."
You cannot couple annihilation with *abiding wrath.* The
wrath of God abideth on men because they are guilty of
eternal sin, and so in the last chapter of our Bible we hear the
seer saying, "He that is unrighteous, let him be unrighteous
still more: and he which is filthy, let him be filthy still more:
and he that is righteous, let him be righteous still more: and
he that is holy, let him be holy still more" (Rev. 22:11, R.V.,
margin). Character tends to permanency.

> "Sow a thought, you reap an act;
> Sow an act, you reap a habit;
> Sow a habit, you reap a character;
> Sow a character, you reap a destiny."

God meant men to understand, and it seems to me there

can be no question about it, that if men die in their sins, there is no hope that they will ever be brought into a state of harmony with Him whose grace they have spurned, or with the Saviour whose blood they have trampled under foot. And so we read, "It is a fearful thing to fall into the hands of the living God" (Hebrews 10:31). I know we live in a namby-pamby age when men make light of iniquity, but according to the Word of God, sin is a fearful affront to the Divine Majesty. To be uncleansed from sin means to die in sin, exist forever in sin, and be banished eternally from the presence of a holy God.

But, thank God, this is still the day of His grace. One would shrink from proclaiming a truth like this, if he were not permitted to proclaim the other truth: "He that believeth on the Son *hath* everlasting life," and so today, if you are unsaved, you may have eternal life by believing on the Lord Jesus Christ. To believe on Him is to trust Him, rest your whole soul upon Him as your Saviour, and take Him as your Redeemer.

> "My Redeemer, oh what beauties
>   In that lovely Name appear;
> None but Jesus in His glories
>   Shall the honored title wear;
> My Redeemer! oh, how sweet to call Thee mine.
>
> "Sunk in ruin, sin and misery,
>   Bound by Satan's captive chain;
> Guided by his artful treach'ry,
>   Hurrying on to endless pain,
> My Redeemer plucked me as a brand from hell."

You can say this if you will come to Christ today.

Chapter IV

DREAMS THAT WILL NEVER COME TRUE

"And the multitude of all the nations that fight against
Ariel, even all that fight against her and her munition,
and that distress her, shall be as a dream of a night
vision. It shall even be as when an hungry man dreameth, and, behold, he eateth; but he awaketh, and his soul
is empty: or as when a thirsty man dreameth, and, behold, he drinketh; but he awaketh, and, behold, he is
faint, and his soul hath appetite: so shall the multitude
of all nations be that fight against mount Zion" (Isaiah
29:7, 8).

IT is a recognized principle in homiletics, that is, the science of preaching, that the preacher should never take a
text for a pretext, and yet I apprehend that is what I
will be charged with doing now, for I do not call attention to
this passage of Scripture with the thought of emphasizing
its primary meaning, but rather to enforce a very important
lesson.

Actually, this twenty-ninth chapter of Isaiah refers to an
incident in Israel's history, when Sennacherib and the Assyr-
ian host gathered about Jerusalem and vainly thought that
they would be able to destroy the city, sweep it out of existence, put the people of Israel to death, or carry them into
captivity; and so Jehovah contemplates the enemies as coming
down upon their prey. Already it seems to them that their
purpose is accomplished. Jerusalem seems to be utterly de-
fenseless against them, but the word of Jehovah, who has
never forsaken His people, and who never will forsake those
that put their trust in Him, says that they are not to be afraid
of this great host, for all their evil thoughts will come to

naught, and all their unholy ambitions will end in disappointment. "It shall be as when an hungry man dreameth, and, behold, he eateth; but he awaketh and his soul is empty: or as when a thirsty man dreameth, and, behold, he drinketh; but he awaketh, and, behold, he is faint, and his soul hath appetite: so shall the multitude of all the nations be that fight against mount Zion." That is, their dream of overcoming Israel would never be fulfilled.

But I am not going to occupy you with this thought, except to say that there is coming another day in the history of Israel when they will be in dire straits similar to these. They are already thronging back to Palestine, and have very bright hopes before them, but they will still have to face that sad and terrible time of Jacob's trouble, called the great tribulation, the like of which they have never known in the past and never shall know again. Once more the Gentile powers will be gathered against Jerusalem and will seek to destroy the people of God, but again Jehovah will come to their defense and the Gentile nations will be disappointed, and their dream of destroying Jerusalem and the Jewish people will prove to be utterly unreal.

World Dreams

There are so many dreams that will never be fulfilled—that will never come true. First, there is the dream of finding heart satisfaction and soul rest in the things of this poor world. Have you been dreaming a dream like that? There are many different aspects of that dream. Some people imagine that they can find lasting enjoyment and true pleasure in a low vulgar life of abominable sensuality, and they fling to the winds decency and self-respect, and go down to the lowest depths of carnality and iniquity. Is there any real good to be found in a life like that? If you have tried it, you know in the deepest depths of your soul that you found nothing but sorrow and bitter disappointment. The incurable disease wards in our great hospitals all over this land tell what a wretched blunder men make when they try to find satisfaction or happiness in sensual living, "receiving in themselves that recompense of their error which was meet." If there is a young man or young woman who has so far forgotten what is true and right and pure as to imagine that it makes little or no difference if you swing loose from the restraints of decency and allow yourself to fall into unclean living, and imagine you are ministering to the desire for happiness, some day you will wake up to find it is a horrid dream, "As when an hungry man dreameth, and, behold, he eateth: but he awaketh, and his soul is empty." There is no satisfaction to be found in sensuality.

Dreams of Worldly Pleasures

On the other hand, there are many who would look with abhorrence or disgust on any such life, but imagine they are going to find happiness and contentment in the respectable pleasures of this world. These people are of a different character to the grossly sensual. But tens of thousands, yes, millions have tried this before you, and not one man or woman has ever yet found heart rest in the things of this poor world. "All that is in the world, the lust of the flesh, and the lust of the eye, and the pride of life, is not of the Father, but is *of the world;* and the world passeth away, and the lust thereof: but he that doeth the will of God abideth for ever" (1 John 2:16, 17). That is why the world can never satisfy the human heart.

There is a striking passage in Ecclesiastes, in which Solomon tells us how he tried everything that his day had to offer, only to exclaim at length, "Vanity of vanities; all is vanity" (Ecclesiastes 1:2). He gives the reason why the world cannot satisfy men: "He hath set eternity in their heart" (Ecclesiastes 3:11, R.V.). The Authorized Version does not bring this out; it reads: "He hath set the world in their heart." But the original Hebrew really means "eternity." How can a man created for eternity ever be satisfied with the things of this world? The old Puritans had a rather nice conception of it; they said, "The world is round; the human heart is three-cornered; you can never fill a three-cornered heart with a round world." We sometimes use the figure of a triangle to represent the triune God, and so they used to say, "It takes a triune God to fill a triangular heart to overflowing."

You may be trying to find satisfaction in the world. I can understand that, for I tried it myself. I know something of the meaning of the hymn:

> "O Christ, in Thee my soul hath found,
>   And found in Thee alone,
> The peace, the joy I sought so long,
>   The bliss till now unknown.
>
> "Now, none but Christ can satisfy,
>   None other Name for me;
> There's love, and life, and lasting joy,
>   Lord Jesus, found in Thee!
>
> "I tried the broken cisterns, Lord,
>   But, ah! the waters failed;
> E'en as I stooped to drink they fled,
>   And mocked me as I wailed.
>
> "The pleasures lost I sadly mourned,
>   But never wept for Thee,
> Till grace my sightless eyes received,
>   Thy loveliness to see.'

Then I found a satisfaction that has lasted now for forty years, and it will last for all eternity. No, there is nothing in the world that will satisfy the human heart. The man who imagines that this world will meet the cravings of his soul, will some day wake up to find that he has just been dreaming, imagining he was finding peace and satisfaction, but his soul will be empty.

Dreams of World Wealth

There are some who dream that if they could just get a sufficient amount of money, they would be satisfied. Did you ever see any one who had enough money to satisfy him? Some years ago a newspaper offered a prize for the best definition for *money*. The answer that won the prize was this: "Money is a universal provider for everything but happiness." Men may have millions, but money cannot satisfy the soul. The man who imagines he will find heart satisfaction in wealth is doomed to wake up at last bitterly disappointed.

Some imagine they will find peace and satisfaction in fame, in the plaudits of their fellows. But the great of earth, those whose names have become household words, would be the most lonely men of their time if they did not know Christ. No, dear friend, try what you will, you will never find lasting peace outside of Christ.

A Beautiful Young Woman Saved

A number of years ago I was holding special meetings in the First Baptist Church of Los Gatos, California. On my first Sunday morning there, the text was: "Whosoever drinketh of this water shall thirst again: but whosoever drinketh of the water that I shall give him shall never thirst; but the water that I shall give him shall be in him a well of water springing up into everlasting life" (John 4:13, 14). Sitting in the front pew was a young woman whose pale, emaciated face and great dark hungry eyes attracted my attention. She listened so earnestly. After the meeting I said to the pastor:

"Who was the very sickly but intensely beautiful young woman who sat in the front pew?"

"She is a very well bred girl," he replied, "but some years ago she threw Christianity to the winds. She was brought up in a Christian home. She went in for a worldly career, trying to find satisfaction and peace in the things of the world, but within the last five months she has been stricken with that dread disease of tuberculosis, and she has the kind that we call galloping consumption. She has not long to live; she is losing strength day after day, and the doctor says she will soon be gone; and now she is wretched and miserably unhappy."

I prayed for her, and each night I would find myself looking through that audience, hoping she would be there, listening to the gospel, but I never saw her at another meeting. About three weeks later a lady came to me, and said: "Do you remember meeting Miss H——?" I remembered that it was this young woman, and she added, "She is very ill, dying of tuberculosis. She heard you the first time you spoke, and was expecting to attend all the meetings, but she has been too ill. She has sent for you."

"I will be glad to go," was my reply. So we went to the room in which she sat. She excused herself for not standing to greet us, for she was too weak. I said, "I am glad you have sent for me."

"She looked up and said, "Mr. Ironside, the doctor told me yesterday that I have just three weeks to live, and I am not saved. I would like to know Christ. Do you think He will take a girl who rejected Him, deliberately turned her back on Him in health, now that I am bitterly disappointed, and everything I have counted on has gone by the board? Do you think there is any hope for a sinner like me?"

You know things look differently when you realize you have only three weeks to live! Many a one, careless now, would be in dead earnest if he knew that within three weeks he would have to face God and eternity.

"Well," I said, "I understand that you have had a very happy life in some respects; you have been very much sought after and admired by the world."

"Oh, please do not talk of that now," she said, "I am afraid I have been selling my soul for worldly popularity. I thought I was going to find happiness and enjoyment, but now it gives me no peace, no satisfaction, to look back over those years of popularity, those years of worldly pleasure. Only three weeks and I must give an account to God, and I am not saved."

It was a real joy to my own soul to open the Word of God and show her how the blessed Lord Jesus in infinite grace had come all the way from heaven's fullest glory down to Calvary's deepest depths of woe for her redemption, and if she would put her heart trust in Him, confess her guilt, she would have all the past blotted out. Directing her to John 3:18, I read: "He that believeth on him is not condemned: but he that believeth not is condemned already, because he hath not believed in the name of the only begotten Son of God." And then I put the question to her, "Tell me, do you believe the Lord Jesus Christ is the Son of God?"

"I do."

Then I asked, "Do you believe that God the Father sent Him into this world to die for sinners?"

"Yes, it is in the Bible; I do believe it," she replied.

"Do you believe He meant you when He said: 'Him that cometh to me I will in no wise cast out'?" I asked.

"It is for everybody, isn't it?" she said.

"Yes," I replied, " 'For God so loved the world, that he gave his only begotten Son, that whosoever believeth in him should not perish, but have everlasting life' (John 3:16). Are you included in that *whosoever?*"

"Yes," she said, "I believe I am."

"Then tell me," I said, "what does the Lord Jesus Christ say about you? Look at verse eighteen again; notice there are only two classes of people there: the first class, 'he that believeth on him,' and the second class, 'he that believeth not.' Notice there is something predicated of the first class and something of the second class. Of the first it is said, 'He that believeth is not condemned'; and of the second, 'He that believeth not is condemned already.' Now before I ask you to tell me which class you are in, let us bow in prayer."

She could not kneel, but her friend and I knelt in prayer. We asked God by the Spirit to open His Word and bring it home in power to her soul.

"Read it again," I said.

"Do you see the two classes? Which one are you in?"

She was silent for a long time as we knelt there before God, and then she looked up, the tears glistening in her beautiful eyes, and she said, "I am in the first class."

"How do you know?"

"Because I do believe in Him. It doesn't say He won't take me in because I come so late. I have come, and I do believe in Him."

"And what is true of you?" I asked.

She looked at it and whispered, "Not condemned!"

I said, "Is that enough to meet God on?"

She replied, "That will do; not condemned!"

Three weeks from eternity, but resting upon the Word of God! I saw her only twice again, and then my meetings ended. About five weeks later I met the Baptist preacher on the street, and he said, "You remember Miss H—? Do you know that just twenty-one days from the day you led her to Christ, I was called to her bedside, and I found her just slipping away."

"Can you hear me?" I asked.

"Yes," she said.

"Do you believe on the Lord Jesus Christ?"

"Yes," she answered.

"And what does He say about you?" I asked.

"Not condemned!" and then she whispered, "If you see Mr. Ironside, tell him, 'Not condemned!' It is all right."

Oh, I tell you, dear friend, that was something real, because that young woman had the Word of the living God to rest upon; but there are many who rest upon their own imaginations instead of resting upon God's immutable Word.

Still Other Dreams

Another dream that will never come true is the dream that if you do the best you can, if you live a respectable life, if you join the church, if you give your money for the cause of Christ, then, when you die, you will go to heaven on your own merit. That is the worst dream of all, and in eternity men who have died trusting in something of that character will be "Even as when an hungry man dreameth, and, behold, he eateth: but he awaketh, and his soul is empty."

Mark this! God has provided the bread of life whereby, if a man eat thereof, he shall live forever. The Lord Jesus Christ said, "I am the living bread which came down from heaven: if any man eat of this bread, he shall live forever: and the bread that I will give is my flesh, which I will give for the life of the world" (John 6:51). What is it to *eat Christ?* It is this, receive Him into your inmost being. Just as you take food and receive it into your physical body, so take Christ. When by faith you receive Him into your own life and heart, you are eating the living bread, and will never waken to find out that this is all a dream.

People of the world think that Christians are dreamers. Thirty years ago when I was a Salvation Army officer, they

were having a street meeting, and a poor fellow who had
been deep in sin, but wonderfully converted, was standing
out on the street telling what the Lord had done for him.
A great big burly man in the crowd suddenly shouted out:
"Wake up, old man, wake up; you're dreaming!"

At that a little girl stepped up to him, and said, "Oh,
please, sir, please don't wake him up. That is my daddy, and
he is such a good daddy now. But he used to be so different
before he began to "dream," as you call it. He was always
beating mother, he spent all his money for drink, and we
were so miserable; but when he began to "dream" like this,
everything was different. He brings his money home now
and provides for us all. He is so kind to mother and to all
of us, and we want him just like he is now."

Oh yes, the world thinks it is the Christian, the believer,
who is the dreamer, but we know that it is the Christ-rejector who is dreaming. The unsaved man who hopes that
everything is going to come out all right, when in reality
it is all wrong, and will be so, for all eternity, unless he turns
to Christ, is the real dreamer. Be persuaded that there is
no other Saviour but Jesus; there is no other way but His
way. Do you want to know the Saviour? You have tried
the world, and imagined you could find peace and happiness
in what it had to offer you. May it not be that today God is
awakening you out of your dreams? You have never found
peace in the world, and you never will. Why not come to
Christ?

> "While we pray, and while we plead,
> While you see your soul's deep need;
> While your Father calls you home,
> Will you not, my brother, come?"

CHAPTER V

THE CHAINS OF SIN

"And he smote Peter on the side, and raised him up, saying, Arise up quickly. And his chains fell off from his hands" (Acts 12:7).

LET me draw your attention to a most interesting incident, recorded in Acts 12:1-19. However, I do not intend to consider it from a merely historical standpoint, but as a remarkable illustration of man's lost condition, and God's marvelous salvation. I want you to think of Peter, not as an apostle, nor as an eminent servant of Christ, but as a picture of any poor lost sinner. We notice six things predicated of Peter which are true of every unconverted man.

First, we see him in *bondage*. He is captive to a tyrant, determined upon his destruction. Are you out of Christ, and do you think that you are free, and sometimes look with pity upon Christians because you imagine they are in bondage to certain ancient ideas which keep them from enjoying themselves in the world, the way you fancy you are enjoying yourself? The Jews of Christ's day boldly declared that they were never in bondage to any man, but Jesus said, "The servant of sin is the slave of sin." They were in bondage to sin and Satan, and that is true of every unconverted person. The unbeliever is deceived by the devil; he is captive to his will. You may say, "I am not going to give up my will to some one else," but you have already done that very thing. If you are unsaved, you are a captive to the god and prince of this world, and what is more you cannot deliver yourself, you cannot set yourself free.

In the second place, Peter was *guarded*. Herod had guards

stationed to watch and see that he did not get away. He was delivered to four quaternions of soldiers. I do not know the actual names of those soldiers, but I have an idea of what they suggest. One of them might suggest *pride,* another *procrastination,* a third, *sinful pleasure,* and the last, *the love of the world;* for I know that these are the means that Satan uses to guard men, and keep them in their sins, and hinder them from getting deliverance. How many there are who would have come to Christ years ago but for the pride of the human heart—too proud to acknowledge their lost condition, to confess their sins, to admit their wrong. "Pride goeth before destruction, and a haughty spirit before a fall."

The Indian Prince

I heard a story years ago which illustrates the folly of pride.

There were two Hindu princes in conflict one with another. One had been defeated, and his son taken captive. The victorious Rajah was going to march into the city in triumph, with a great string of captives walking barefoot before the great elephant upon which he was mounted. This young prince was brought before him, and told that he was to strip off his royal garments and walk barefoot with the other captives. He was very indignant, and exclaimed, "What kind of faces will the people make when they see me, a prince, walking like that?"

"You have not yet heard it all," said the Rajah, "you shall not only walk barefoot in this procession, but you will carry a bowl of milk that will be filled almost to the brim, and if you spill one drop of it, off comes your head. I shall have guards to see whether you spill any or not."

The prince turned deadly pale as he heard that. As the procession was arranged. they handed him the bowl of milk.

You can imagine his predicament. The procession started. How carefully this young prince walked! But in some way or another he managed to get through without spilling a drop. When he was brought before the Rajah, he was sternly asked: "Well, what kind of faces did the people make?"

"O sire," said the poor prince, "I saw no one's face; I saw only my life that I held in my hands, and I knew that if I dared to look to the right or to the left, it would be forfeited."

O friend, you are a poor sinner exposed to the judgment of God, but now offered a free and full salvation through infinite grace. Are you too proud to be saved on God's terms, too proud to humble yourself and admit your lost condition? Are you more concerned about what men think than what God thinks? How well the devil knows how to guard his subjects!

Other Prison Guards

Then there is that other guard, *procrastination.* "The road of By-and-By leads to the town of Never." A great many people are not saved, because they are always saying, "There is plenty of time," and the devil puts old Captain Procrastination on duty to guard them, and if they get exercised, he says to the young, "There is plenty of time; you are young yet." To those in middle life, he says, "Go on and make your fortune, then you can think about your soul." But old age comes and they are still in their sins. The time for them is gone, and they pass into eternity—lost. "The harvest is past, the summer is ended, and we are not saved" (Jeremiah 8:20).

How well Satan knows how to use the third and fourth guards—*the pleasures of sin* and *the love of the world*—to keep people from coming to Christ. If they bestir themselves and are anxious to be saved, these guards are there to say, "You will lose all your good times, if you become a Christian; you will have to be long-faced and you will be miserable and wretched. You won't be able to go to this, or to that; you won't be able to enjoy this or that; put it off; wait until the world has lost its charm." And so, because men love the world and think more of the pleasures of sin than they do of their eternal salvation, they remain in bondage—some of them until it is too late to be saved.

Peter's Dire Condition

Then notice the third thing: Peter was in *darkness*. That is the condition of every one by nature: "Having the understanding darkened, being alienated from the life of God through the ignorance that is in them, because of the blindness of their heart" (Ephesians 4:18). You cannot see in the dark. How often you will hear this said, "I have heard of this salvation for years, but I cannot see how God can save a sinner through the death of His Son; I cannot see how the blood of Christ can wash away my guilt; I cannot understand how I can be sure that the Bible is the Word of God?" Of course you cannot! You are in darkness, and what you need is light. The great apostle to the Gentiles declares, "But if our gospel be hid, it is hid to them that are lost: in whom the god of this world hath blinded the minds of them which believe not, lest the light of the glorious gospel of Christ, who is the image of God, should shine unto them" (2 Corinthians 4:3, 4). If you make the confession, "I cannot see; I cannot understand how the blood of Jesus can wash away my sin," that is all that is needed to tell the true condition of your soul. You are in the dark, away from God, and in dire need of a Saviour.

Then notice something else: Peter was not only in bondage, guarded, and in darkness, but he was *sound asleep*. That is the condition of men in their sins today. But the voice of

God sounds forth: "Awake thou that sleepest, and arise from the dead, and Christ shall give thee light" (Ephesians 5:14). The business of the evangelist is to go to men, asleep in their sins, and awaken them. Real hard sleepers do not like to be awakened. I have two boys, and both of them, when they were at a certain growing age, did like to stay up late at night; but oh, how hard it was to get them up in the morning! What a job it was to awaken them. Listen to the sleeper in Proverbs, "Yet a little sleep, a little slumber, a little folding of the hands to sleep" (Proverbs 6:10). My friend, a little more sleep and you will awaken in hell to sleep no more for all eternity! It is only the omnipotent power of God that can awaken poor sleeping sinners.

Then there is something else: Peter was *bound* with two chains. Are you bound with the chains of your sin? You may remember the story of the Grecian tyrant, who looked with suspicion upon a certain metal worker, who was able to make the finest chains of any man in his dominions. This tyrant had an idea that the man was a traitor against his government. One day he sent for him, and after flattering him, said, "I understand there is no one in my kingdom that can make as fine or as strong a chain as you can. Let me see you make one." With the tyrant looking on, the smith made a magnificent chain. He finished it, and as he handed it over to the tyrant, he said, "If you were to take two elephants, and fasten one to each end of this chain, they could not tear it apart."

The tyrant said, "Are you certain of that?"

"Absolutely," the man replied.

Then, turning to two of his officers, the tyrant said, "Take him and bind him with it, and cast him into prison." He was bound with the very chain he had made.

Sinner, you have been forging a chain, the chain of your sins, link by link throughout the years, and if you are not saved soon, you are going to be bound with that chain, and be cast into that awful place "prepared for the devil and his angels." You will have no one to blame but yourself. You will remember how you forged that chain, link by link; how you fell into this or that particular sin, and then said to yourself, "Oh, well, I will not repeat it; I will do it just once." Then in some way there was an unaccountable urge to commit the same sin again and again and again, and you found out at last that you were forging the links in the chain that has bound your soul. You have tried and tried to break it, but you are not able to do it.

Chains that Bind

You know what chains are binding *your* soul today. The awful chains of lust, untruthfulness, pride, infidelity, dishonesty, greed, and unbelief. These are the things that are going to bind men's souls for eternity, and sink them down into outer darkness. It is said of the fallen angels that they are bound in everlasting chains under darkness; and that will be true also of men and women who reject Christ.

The chains of sin! You remember how you tried to break them! On New Year's Day, you said, "Now I am going to swear off; I am not going to commit this sin or that sin any more. I am losing my will-power; these things have robbed me of my self respect; I am ashamed to think of the habits of which no one knows, but myself and God; I will surely break loose." And you tried and tried, and then fell back into the same old ways.

Or, you may have said, "It is of no use to try; I cannot free myself; I am bound with chains that I cannot break." And so far as your own strength is concerned, that is perfectly true. But that is not the whole story. What have we seen of Peter? We have seen that he was a captive; he was guarded by Satan's soldiers; he was wrapped in darkness; he

was sound asleep; he was bound with chains; and there is
one other word to complete the vivid description, he was
under sentence of *death,* condemned already. There he lies
in that prison, a picture of any poor sinner.

Why was the sentence against Peter not carried out?
Herod was waiting until a more propitious time, when he
was going to bring him before the people and put him to
death. That suggests what God says about you, if you are
still rejecting the Lord Jesus Christ. "He that believeth on
him is not condemned: but he that believeth not is condemned
already, because he hath not believed in the name of the
only begotten Son of God" (John 3:18). Notice, that you
are not merely in danger of being condemned in the day of
judgment; not only in danger of condemnation, if you die
rejecting Christ; but you are *condemned already.* And why?
Because you are even now a Christ-rejector. "He that believeth not is condemned already." Again in John 3:36, we
read, "He that believeth on the Son hath everlasting life:
and he that believeth not the Son shall not see life; but the
wrath of God abideth on him." Just as the wrath of Herod
was abiding on Peter, and he was waiting the time for the
sentence to be carried out, so the wrath of a righteous God
abides upon the Christ-rejector, and soon the sentence will
be carried out.

Deliverance Through Prayer

But now a word to Christians: You are interested in sinners, you know they are in the darkness, you understand that
they are captives of Satan, bound by the chains of their sins,
guarded, and under condemnation, and yet you have a re-
source, have you not? The people of God offered prayer to
God continually for Peter's deliverance. O Christian, be
encouraged when you pray for those in bondage. The ear
of God is open to your cry. There are dear boys and girls

who are still unsaved, and you realize they are in the dark; you long that they should be brought to the light. Keep on praying for them! As the saints prayed for Peter, God wrought; as we pray for sinners, God saves today!

What happened as they prayed for Peter? Seven things took place.

First, as they were praying, a messenger from God came to Peter. You know how often God does just that very thing. Sometimes he sends a human messenger, sometimes a word from the Book, sometimes conviction by the Holy Spirit. Peter was sound asleep, and suddenly there appeared a messenger. The angel of the Lord is able to awaken, to arouse, to give deliverance to those who desire to be delivered.

Second, a light shone in the prison. It is the truth of God that dispels the darkness. "The entrance of thy words giveth light; it giveth understanding unto the simple" (Psalm 119:130). The messenger came, and the light shone! O unsaved sinner, have you heard the gospel message, the message of light? You say in your darkness, "I cannot see; I cannot understand." Listen! "This is a faithful saying, and worthy of all acceptation, that Christ Jesus came into the world to save sinners; of whom I am chief" (1 Timothy 1:15). Does that not give you a little light? "Verily, verily, I say unto you, he that heareth my word, and believeth on him that sent me, hath everlasting life, and shall not come into condemnation; but is passed from death unto life" (John 5:24). This is God's own Word. May it bring light to your darkened mind.

Third, the angel smote Peter on the side. He was a real "Billy" Sunday. Some folk do not like "Billy's" abrupt way, but in this case the situation was desperate, and the angel said, "Wake up," as he smote him, and Peter wakened to find the angel pounding him. Some of us remember how the Spirit laid hold on us, and aroused us from our death-like sleep. The Word came home with convicting power, and we were saved. I would to God that you, unsaved one, might be smitten by the convicting power of the Spirit of God, that you might realize your lost condition, and your need of a Saviour; and that you would turn to Him who awakens, and be delivered.

Fourth, there was no resistance on Peter's part. The message came, "Get up!" and Peter obeyed immediately. Why, you know, a little while before, that word would have meant nothing to him; but now he is awake. When men and women are awakened, the message comes: "Believe the Word; arise, He calleth thee."

Fifth, then his chains fell off. Do you want to be delivered from your chains? Believe the Word! I have a friend who years ago was a victim of that dreadful habit of smoking and eating opium. He had fallen into that vice when very young, and the thing had gotten such a grip on him that he could not break it. At last, at twenty-two years of age, he was such a wreck that he had made up his mind that he might as well end it all by suicide, for there was no hope for him. But one night in Fresno, California, he was going down the street, crying out, "What a fool I have been to form a habit like this that I cannot free myself from," when he heard a little group of Salvation Army folk singing,

> "He breaks the power of canceled sin,
>   He sets the prisoner free;
> His blood can make the vilest clean,
>   His blood avails for me."

He said, "What's that?" They sang it again. That poor young fellow stood there trembling, for he had hardly strength enough to stand erect. "I wonder if it is true— 'the vilest'—that's me!" and he followed them into their hall. When they invited sinners to come to Christ, he went forward and knelt at the penitent bench, but he was so loathsome that they said, "Oh, he is too far gone." However, they were faithful, and knelt with him and pointed him to Christ. By and by, as he arose, he said, "I will trust Him," and went away. One of them said to another, "You better go and see if he has any lodging tonight; he has no will power, there is no hope for him, if he gets away." Somebody did take an interest in him; he got him a lodging, and helped him in other ways. When he put his trust in Christ, he was delivered, and he has often testified since, "I am free; Christ has delivered me; I never even had a struggle to get rid of that habit." In two weeks you would not have known him. He was a new creature, physically, mentally, and every way. Whatever your sins are, come to Christ, trust in Him, and find deliverance. Peter's bonds fell off; he was freed from his chains—you too may be free.

Sixth, "Get your things on," the angel said, and he dressed him up. That is what the Lord does. Off with the prison garments, on with the new garments. Then they went through one door and another, and finally through the great iron door. If Peter had gone through that great iron door in his chains, he would have gone through to die. If he were taken through in his fetters, he would go out to be executed. And if you go through the door of death in your sins, you go through to your doom. Peter might well have trembled as he passed through that door, if he still had his chains on; but as he drew near, the door opened of its own accord, and he went through as a free man. A believer in the Lord Jesus can say, "I have died already; I am free!" You may ask, "How can you say that?" "Well, we have been crucified with Christ; we went through death with Him!"

Seventh, then Peter said, "I must hunt up some place where I can find some Christians who are interested in me." They were all having a prayer meeting in Mary's house, praying for Peter's deliverance. The Lord had answered and he was delivered, but they were still praying. A little girl came out in response to Peter's knock, and she got so excited when she heard his voice, that she forgot to open the door. She rushed back, and said, "You don't need to pray any more; Peter is outside, he is at the door!"

"Nonsense," they practically said, "God doesn't do anything as quickly as that."

Is that not just like us? Sometimes we pray and pray, and when God answers, we can hardly believe it. But she insisted, "I *know* he is there."

"It is his ghost," they said, "he has gone through in his chains, and that is his ghost."

"Well," she replied, "there is no use arguing; come and see!" And to the door they went where Peter continued knocking!

What an illustration this is, dear unsaved one, of God's salvation. Have you seen your own picture? Have you been asleep in your sins? Are you in darkness and guarded by Satan? Do you want to be delivered? Listen to the Word of God, and do not be angry if the Spirit of God has to smite you. Believe the Word, act upon it, and you will enter into the fullness of blessing. You will be delivered from the chains of your sins.

Chapter VI

THE SINLESS ONE MADE SIN

> "For he hath made him to be sin for us, who knew no
> sin; that we might be made the righteousness of God
> in him" (2 Corinthians 5:21).

I WANT you to consider with me one of the great texts
of the Bible, a verse that brings before us the most remarkable transaction that has ever taken place in the
universe, when the holy, spotless Son of God took the sinner's place, and offered up Himself in expiation of our sins.
Let me ask you to think first for a few minutes of the meaning of the words, "He knew no sin." After that we will meditate upon the expression, "He was made sin," and then we
will consider the rest of the verse, "That we might be made
the righteousness of God in him."

"He knew no sin." These words suggest three things regarding the perfection of the humanity of our Lord Jesus
Christ. In the first place, He never made the acquaintance
of sin by actual disobedience to the law of God. He never
swerved from the path of rectitude in the slightest particular. In all His life down here, He was ever the unsinning
one. "He did no sin, neither was guile found in his mouth."
He could turn to His bitterest enemies, and ask without the
slightest hesitation, or fear that they would dare attempt to
answer, "Which of you convinceth me of sin?" Neither
they nor any of the thousands since who have investigated
the records have ever been able to point to one flaw in His
behavior.

"He knew no sin" means that He never committed sin,
and in this He stands apart from other men; for of every

other it is written, "All have sinned, and come short of the glory of God." Therefore the need of repentance. "God commandeth all men everywhere to repent," for all men have dishonored Him and are guilty in His sight. But our blessed Lord never repented of anything. He never retracted a word He said. He never confessed the slightest failure. He never apologized for anything. He was never sorry for any act or word. He never lifted His heart to God in confession of failure.

Let me ask you, if you profess to be a Christian, how did your life of piety begin? Did it not start with repentance? When you first came to God, did you not bow before Him a penitent, confessing your sins, and seeking forgiveness because of your iniquities? In the case of every godly man or woman, contrition and confession have a large place. But how different was the piety of our Lord Jesus Christ. As Bushnell so strikingly expresses it, "In Him you see piety without one dash of repentance." He never shed a tear because of His blunders or mistakes. He never on any occasion recalled one thing He ever said. His most devoted followers failed: Peter denied Him; James and John would have called down fire from heaven upon those who refused the ministry of their Master; Thomas doubted Him; Philip questioned; Paul brought railing accusations against the high priest in Israel, and immediately afterward apologized for it; Barnabas lost his temper; Mark proved untrustworthy on more than one occasion. But our blessed Lord moved on in perfect serenity through every experience of life. He was the sinless One. And yet He was truly man, but He was more than man. He was God incarnate, and therefore absolutely without sin.

No Confession to Make

Notice the prayer life of our blessed Lord. Because He

became man, He prayed to the Father. He took the place of a dependent. He trod the path of faith, and drew His strength from above. He was often found at night on a hillside, or in a garden, pouring out His heart in prayer. But His prayer never took the character of confession. Hence He always prayed alone. He never prayed in fellowship with any one else. He prayed *for* others. He did not pray *with* them. We never find Him kneeling with Peter, James, and John, His intimate disciples, and joining together with them in intercession, nor with any one else. We who serve Christ today have some of our most blessed experiences as we mingle our prayers and supplications with those of our brethren, and bow together before God in acknowledgment of our common sinfulness and our common need. He never did this with any one. He taught His disciples to pray, "Forgive us our trespasses, as we forgive those who trespass against us," but He could not, in the very nature of things, pray that prayer with them. He stood altogether apart. They were sinners; He was sinless, the Saviour of sinners. *"He knew no sin."*

The Word of God teaches that He not only never made the acquaintance of sin, by actual failure, by transgression, by disobedience in thought, word, or deed, but He knew no sin in the sense that His humanity was never contaminated by an inward tendency to sin. He was absolutely, from the moment of His incarnation, the holy One. The angel said to the blessed virgin mother: "That holy thing which shall be born of thee shall be called the Son of God." In Adam, unfallen, we see humanity *innocent;* in all his children since, we see humanity *fallen;* but in Christ Jesus we see humanity *holy.* We are told that He was tempted in all points like as we are, yet without sin. Some people have taken this last expression to mean, "Yet without sinning." That was true as we have seen, but it is not all of the truth. That verse really means this: He was tempted in all points like as we are, apart from sin. He was never tempted by inbred sin. He could say, "The prince of this world cometh, and hath nothing in me." You cannot say that; I cannot. When the enemy comes at me from without, there is a traitor inside who would gladly surrender the citadel, if he could; but with my Lord it was quite otherwise.

Tempted in All Points

If any ask how He could be tempted in all points like as we are, if He did not possess a sinful nature, I would remind you that our first parents were sinless when temptation first came to them. They were tested on three points, the lust of the flesh, the lust of the eye, and the pride of life. These are the only three ways in which man can be tested. Temptation either comes in the form of fleshly suggestion, the temptation of the body; or, it comes along esthetical lines, the temptation of the soul; or, it appeals to the mind, the temptation of the spirit. When Eve looked upon the tree, she saw that its fruit was good for food—the lust of the flesh; that it was pleasant to the eyes—the lust of the eye; that it was desired to make one wise—the pride of life. She capitulated on every point. Adam shared in her sin, and thus the race became fallen. To Christ in the wilderness among the wild beasts, Satan said, "Make these stones bread." It was the appeal to the lust of the flesh. He showed our Lord all the kingdoms of earth and the glory of them—the lust of the eye. He suggested His leaping from the pinnacle of the temple to be sustained by angel hands and thus be accredited to the people—the pride of life. But each temptation failed, even as an arrow is turned back by a steel plate. He was without sin. He suffered being tempted. The very presentation of temptation to Him was in itself so obnoxious that it caused Him the keenest suffering. It is the very opposite generally with us. Peter tells us that "He that hath suffered in the flesh hath ceased from sin." Sin in our eyes is alluring. It is presented to us as something attractive and delightful. Our corrupt natures respond to the temptation from without, and we have to suffer in the flesh in order to resist. But it was never so with Him. He suffered when sin in any form was presented to Him.

Let me illustrate this. Suppose that a young man of high principles is associated with his own father in the management of a bank. He loves and honors his father, and nothing means more to him than his father's success, and the recognition of his integrity by his business associates. But suppose some one in the bank should make the suggestion to this son that, if they would act together, they might rob the bank of thousands of dollars, and cover up their wrong-doing temporarily, and be far out of the country before the evil deed could be discovered. Can you imagine the indignation of this young man, and the mental suffering that he would endure, to think that any one would think him capable of doing anything so vile, so low, when he was his father's trusted son? He would be humiliated and ashamed to think that any one would dare to present such a temptation to him. So in a far higher sense, the temptations of our Lord Jesus Christ meant the keenest suffering, for He was absolutely free from all inward tendency to sin.

But we may go farther: "He knew no sin" in the sense that it was unthinkable that He ever could sin, for He was God manifest in the flesh. He did not change His glorious personality when He became man. God the Son from all eternity, became in grace the Son of God, when He was born of a virgin mother, without human father. He was ever the eternal God. Now just as truly as God ex-carnate cannot sin, so He who was God incarnate was absolutely above anything of the kind. If any ask, "How then could His temptation be real, if there was no possibility that He would fall?" the answer is clear and simple—the temptation was not permitted in order to find out if He would fall, but to prove that He would not. It was thus demonstrated that He was an acceptable sin offering.

In the Old Testament we read again and again of the sin offering, "It is most holy." How carefully God manifested this in regard to His Son. The temptation proved it, and then on the very day of His crucifixion distinct testimony was given four times to the same wondrous fact. The wife of Pilate besought her husband, "Have thou nothing to do with the blood of this just one." Pilate himself washed his hands, and said, "I find no fault in him at all." The penitent thief hanging by His side on the cross declared, "This man hath done nothing amiss." When He at last yielded up His spirit to the Father, the Roman centurion exclaimed, "Certainly this was a righteous man." *"He knew no sin."*

"He was made sin." In both the original languages in which the two Testaments were written, the same words were used for sin and sin offering; so we may understand this expression to mean, "He was made the sin offering." We read in Isaiah 53, "When thou shalt make his soul an offering for sin, he shall see his seed, he shall prolong his days, and the pleasure of the Lord shall prosper in his hand." How tremendously solemn! He upon whom the law had no claim whatsoever poured out His soul unto death in the sinner's stead.

Not Physical Suffering Only

Let me remind you that it was not simply the physical suffering which our blessed Lord endured upon the cross that made expiation for iniquity. It was what He suffered in His holy, spotless soul, in His sinless being, when the judgment that our sins deserved fell on Him. For six awful hours

He hung suspended upon that cross. God Himself seems to have divided the time into two halves. From the third to the sixth hour, that is, from nine o'clock in the morning until high noon, according to our way of reckoning, the sun was shining down upon that cross. But from the sixth to the ninth hour, that is, from noon until three o'clock in the afternoon, a supernatural darkness enshrouded the entire scene.

In those first three hours there was no evidence of any special perturbation. He was suffering and agonizing, but He gave no evidence of the least self-pity. Not one word was uttered by those holy lips that indicated for a moment that He was suffering. He looked down at the foot of the cross and saw His mother and John, the beloved, standing near. He said to her, "Behold thy son," and to John, "Behold thy mother." John then took her, and led her away from that awful scene. He looked at the great throng gathered all about Him, and listened to their cries of hatred and blasphemy: "If thou be the Christ, save thyself; come down from the cross." He lifted His heart to the Father and pleaded, "Father, forgive them, for they know not what they do." Then He heard the prayer of the dying malefactor by His side, "Lord, remember me when thou comest into thy kingdom." That was faith. The thief could discern in that thorn-crowned Sufferer, earth's coming glorious King. But Jesus said, as it were, "I will do better than that. You do not need to wait for me to come in my kingdom. 'Today thou shalt be with me in Paradise.'" All His words have to do with the blessing and happiness of others.

During those first three hours, while the sun was shining down upon that cross, He was suffering from the hand of man. But what Jesus endured at the hand of man would never put away one sin. Then suddenly, at high noon, the sun seemed to be blotted out of the heavens. Appalling darkness spread over all the scene. The early Christians used to say that Dionysius the Areopagite was addressing a class of students in Alexandria at that moment, when this supernatural darkness spread over the world, and he suddenly exclaimed, "Either a god is dying, or the universe is about to go into dissolution."

Yes! He who is both God and man was dying. God was then entering into judgment with Him regarding our sins. In those three hours of darkness, darkness which no human eye could pierce, alone upon the cross, the judgment which our sins deserved was visited upon Him. Then His soul was made an offering for sin. Then "He was wounded for our transgressions, he was bruised for our iniquities; the chastisement of our peace was upon him." Then He could cry, as in the words of the Psalmist: "Deep calleth unto deep at the noise of thy water spouts; all thy waves and thy billows are gone over me." Then it was that He was made to be sin for us. In some way that our finite minds can not now understand, the pent-up wrath of the centuries fell upon Him, and He "sank in deep mire where there was no standing," as He endured in His inmost being what you and I would have had to endure through all eternity, had it not been for His mighty sacrifice. Then His soul was made an offering for sin, and as the darkness was passing away, we hear the cry of anguish predicted in the twenty-second Psalm, "My God, my God, why hast thou forsaken me?" Do you know the answer? In order that you and I might have eternal life, He, the holy One, the sinless One, took our place in judgment that we might be forever delivered from condemnation. He went into darkness that light might ever shine upon us. He bore our heavy load of guilt that our sins might be removed as far as the east is from the west.

He is Our Righteousness

"That we might be made the righteousness of God in

Him." We who believe are now through grace the display of divine righteousness; God has shown how He can be just in justifying all who trust in Him who took our place in judgment. Upon the cross our sins were imputed to Him. He endured what we deserved. He drank the bitter cup of wrath which should have been ours. That was the cup from which He shrank in Gethsemane's garden. He could not have been the holy Son had He been able to look upon it with equanimity. But He emptied that cup. He exhausted the wrath of God against our sins, and now divine righteousness demands that all who trust in Him be freed from every charge, and thus fully justified before the throne of God. Seated high in heaven's glory, on the right hand of the Father, He is there as our Representative. His acceptance is ours. God sees us in Him.

Looking back to the cross, the believer can say: "Blessed Lord, there Thou wert made sin for me; there Thou didst bear my judgment; didst endure my desert; I myself am the answer to the cry, 'Why hast thou forsaken me?'"

Looking up to the throne where He now sits exalted, the believer can cry in faith, "Blessed Lord, there upon the throne Thou art my righteousness." This indeed is full salvation, and it is all based upon the blessed fact that "He who knew no sin was made to be sin for us, that we might be made the righteousness of God in him."

Any attempt of ours to provide a righteousness which will satisfy God is doomed to end in failure, yet thousands today who bear the Christian name have never faced their sins before God and found their righteousness in Christ. Nothing is sadder than profession without possession; nothing more solemn than having a name to live, when actually dead in trespasses and in sins. Yet this, alas, is true of all whose hope of salvation is based upon the fact that they have been brought up to respect Christianity, and in a sense to reverence its Founder, but have never taken their place as lost, guilty sinners before God, looked in faith to the Lord Jesus Christ, once made sin for them, and received Him as their own personal Saviour.

Let me affectionately ask you the question, "Have you done so?" Remember that in the life of every one who is saved, there has taken place, at some time or other, that great change described in Scripture as conversion (Matthew 18:3). To be sure, the change is not so marked in some as in others, nor could all point to the day and hour when it occurred; but all who are truly born again have been children of wrath on the road to destruction who came to the place where they received Christ in faith, and thus were saved.

A Religious Woman Lost

Some time ago I heard of a lady living in a country place where modern conveniences in the way of lighting and such like were not to be had. She had never been very wicked, as man would say. Frequently she attended church, said her prayers regularly, even read her Bible, and in short hoped that all was right for eternity, yet was seldom concerned about the question of salvation, for her conscience had never been reached. She had no realization of the sinfulness of her own heart. Wrapped in her rags of self-righteousness she was contentedly hastening on to judgment. Peace in a sense she had, but a false peace, not peace with God. She was simply at peace with herself, for she had never known true soul trouble.

She was alone in her room one night when suddenly the lamp which she had lighted went out, leaving her in the darkness. Almost involuntarily she exclaimed, "There is no oil in the lamp!" Then she added, "I've heard that before. Ah, yes, the parable of the ten virgins (Matthew 25:1-12). Five of them had no oil in their lamps when the bridegroom came, and they were shut out of the feast." Her mind became troubled. For several days and even nights, the thought was ever with her. She would often cry out in anguish of soul, "No, I have no oil in my lamp. My God, what will become of me? I have not the grace of God in my heart!"

A horror of great darkness came upon her. She longed to be saved, yet knew not how. In great distress she began to pray, and God opened her eyes to see her utterly lost, undone condition in His sight, and showed her that she could do nothing to save herself. She searched His Word for light as to how she might obtain the longed-for "oil," and at last was led to realize that the work that saves had all been finished long ago when the Lord Jesus bore her sins in His own body on the tree (1 Peter 2:24); that all she had to do to possess eternal life and to know that she had it, was to believe on Him (1 John 5:13). Glad she was indeed to be saved so simply, and yet in a way that brought such satisfaction. Sin had all been judged on Another, and she was justified from all things (Acts 13:38, 39). She rested in simple faith in Christ, and now rejoices that she is His for time and eternity.

Before, she had a profession; now, she has Christ. Before, she was dressed in the rags of self-righteousness; now, she is clothed in the righteousness of God (1 Corinthians 1:30). Before, she had an empty lamp only; now, she is a possessor of the oil of the Spirit, who has sealed her for heaven (Ephesians 4:30).

Let me earnestly entreat any reader who is without oil in his lamp to face his true condition now, without any further delay. Hesitate not to tell out everything into the ears of a holy God. Then look up by faith to the One who was made to be sin for you, that you might become the righteousness of God in Him. He was lifted up on Calvary's cross "that whosoever believeth on him should not perish, but have eternal life." Saved then by sovereign grace, you will find every need met for time and eternity in the risen Christ, "who of God is made unto us wisdom, and righteousness, and sanctification, and redemption."

CHAPTER VII

TRANSGRESSION FORGIVEN

"Blessed is he whose transgression is forgiven, whose sin is covered. Blessed is the man unto whom the Lord imputeth not iniquity, and in whose spirit there is no guile" (Psalm 32:1, 2).

THOSE who read the Bible with any degree of care, notice that when the apostle Paul quotes from the thirty-second Psalm in the fourth chapter of Romans, showing the great doctrine of justification by faith, it is in perfect accord with the revelation given in the Old Testament. He cites Abraham's case first, a man of whom it was written, "He believed God, and it was counted to him for righteousness," and then says, "Even as David also describeth the blessedness of the man, unto whom God imputeth righteousness without works, saying, Blessed are they whose iniquities are forgiven, and whose sins are covered." So then, the thirty-second Psalm may well be called, as Luther said, a Pauline Psalm. It is in exact accord with the truth set forth in the Epistle to the Romans.

This Psalm is a wonderful record of redeeming grace, and is David's own experience. He is telling how he has been brought into the knowledge of the blessedness of transgression forgiven and sin covered.

You will notice that in the first two verses we have four distinct expressions relating to the blessed man who is right with God.

Blessed is he:

1. Whose transgression is forgiven.
2. Whose sin is covered.
3. Unto whom the Lord imputeth not iniquity.

4. In whose spirit there is no guile.

These four things are true of all believers in our Lord Jesus Christ.

David wrote this long before Christ came into the world. He wrote it as he was looking on in faith to the coming Saviour and His sacrifice. He exclaimed, "Blessed is the man whose transgression is forgiven." He had no thought of God arbitrarily forgiving sins, or passing sin over, as though it were of no moment, but he had in view the work of the Cross, predicted from the very beginning and on down through the ages. You will remember that in Psalm 51, where he makes his great confession, he recognizes the fact that no sacrifice that might be offered upon the Jewish altars could avail to lay the basis of righteousness, but he cries, "Purge me with hyssop, and I shall be clean : wash me, and I shall be whiter than snow." In other words, the thought in David's mind was this, "I cannot offer a sacrifice sufficient to atone for my sins, but on the basis of that sacrifice which Thou Thyself art about to provide, blot out my transgression and pardon my iniquity." So looking on to the Cross, he could exultantly cry, "Blessed is the man whose transgression is forgiven, whose sin is covered," in the sense of being atoned for.

"No Afeard of God Noo"

When I was a boy they used to tell of a lad who lived in the north of Scotland, who was in great distress whenever he thought of meeting God. He was not very bright—the Scotch called him daft. This wee lad was greatly worried whenever he thought of the fact that some day he would have to give account to God for his sins. Many times his elders heard him crying to himself, "Oh, I dinna want to meet God. I am afeard of God. I canna' meet Him."

People tried to comfort him, but they were not able to

make clear to him how anyone could be at peace with God. Finally, in a very simple way, the gospel was explained to the lad, and his joy was unbounded as he saw something of the love and grace of God in giving His Son for him. One day the little fellow was heard crooning to himself, "I am no afeard of God noo, for I am going to heaven noo." Some one said, "Little John, what makes you talk like that? Why are you not afraid of God? Have you not committed sins?"

"Why, I have sinned many times, but I am no afeard of God noo."

"But do you not know that God is righteous and will punish sin?"

"Yes, I have sinned and all that, but I am no afeard of God. He will not punish me."

"Well, what makes you so sure? Can you explain the great doctrine of the atonement?"

Little John scratched his poor, muddled head a moment, and then he said, "Well, some day I am goin' up to meet God, and He will have a big Bible-book in front o' Him, and He will have the sins of all the people written doon in His book. When little John comes up to God, He will turn over the pages of that Bible-book until He finds the one with little John's name on it, but before He can read out the sins, Jesus Christ will be there with His bleeding hand, and He will put it down quick over all the page, and God will look at it, and say, 'I canna find a sin on this page.' The blood will blot them all out, and little John will gang into heaven."

Little John knew more than many of our doctors of divinity, but there was one thing wrong with his theology. We don't wait until the day of judgment for the blood to blot out our sins, but it is done here and now in this world. The moment a poor sinner comes to God owning his guilt and trusting in the Lord Jesus Christ, his sin is atoned for, covered, never to be made manifest again, blotted out forever.

The Word of God is, "As far as the east is from the west, so far hath he removed our transgressions from us." Again God declares, "I have blotted out as a thick cloud thy sins."

It is only through the atoning work of Jesus Christ that God is enabled thus to be just and the justifier of him who believes in Jesus Christ.

Unforgiven Sins Distress

Listen again to what David says, "Blessed is he whose transgression is forgiven, whose sin is covered." He goes on, and tells of the many weeks and months in which his conscience was in great distress because of his sin. "When I kept silence my bones waxed old through my roaring all the day long." There is nothing on earth that will so oppress one, or that will so distress the soul, as a sense of unforgiven sin pressing down upon the conscience. We find in the Scripture, "He that covereth his sins shall not prosper, but whoso confesseth and forsaketh them, shall have mercy."

Have you unforgiven sin resting on your conscience, and have you been hoping to hide it? Be certain that the Word of God is still true: "Be sure your sin will find you out." Some men's sins, we read, are going before them to judgment, and some men they follow after. Some men's sins are so manifest that they can't be hidden. Everyone knows just what they are. Other men manage to keep their sins hidden so that very few on earth know anything about them. By and by, at the judgment bar of God, their sins will seem to leap up and drag their souls to the lowest depths of the pit, when it will be too late to put them away.

Story of Robert Bruce

My heart was stirred as I heard A. H. Stewart tell a story of Scotland's great king, Robert Bruce. On one occasion he was fleeing from the English soldiers of King Edward. They were almost upon him, and he realized he was not maintaining the speed he should, so he left the path and started through the thick forest, hoping to escape. He ran mile after mile thinking that perhaps, at last, he had eluded the vengeance of his foes, when suddenly he heard a sound that caused his heart almost to stand still. It was the baying of his own bloodhounds. He knew the English had let loose his hounds, and put them on their master's track, and the animals which might be supposed to be doing Robert Bruce a favor in running him down, were leading his foes to the place where he was hidden. He knew now that all was over with him, unless he was able to put something between himself and the dogs to throw off the scent. Spent and worn, he toiled on several more weary miles until he came to a clear, rapid, mountain stream. He plunged in and then hastened down the stream a mile or so, and came out on the other side of the forest. There he hid from the sight of his pursuers and listened as the hounds came to the water, and ran up and down, baying and crying out for the scent. The water had washed it away. They were unable to follow their master, and Robert Bruce escaped from the vengeance of the enemy.

O my friends, there is only one stream that will wash out the scent of sin, and that is the precious blood of Christ which cleanseth from all sin. All who come to Jesus, all who trust in Him, are forever free from the judgment which their sins deserve. So David tells us that the time came when it was impossible for him to hide his own sin, impossible to cover his own transgression, and he says, "I acknowledged my sin unto thee, and mine iniquity have I not hid. I said, I will confess my transgressions unto the Lord; and thou forgavest the iniquity of my sin." We read that "If we confess our sins, he is faithful and just to forgive us our sins, and to cleanse us from all unrighteousness" (1 John 1:9).

Precious Hiding Place

Then you will notice as you drop your eyes down to the seventh verse, that he exclaims, as he looks up into the face of God whom he had sinned against, "Thou art my hiding place; thou shalt preserve me from trouble; thou shalt compass me about with songs of deliverance." Think of it! For a long time David had been hiding *from* God, but now we find him hiding *in* God. Which are you doing today? Are you hiding from Him, or have you fled to Him for refuge and found a safe hiding place? We read in the book of the prophet Isaiah, "And a man shall be as an hiding place from the wind, and a covert from the tempest; as rivers of water in a dry place, as the shadow of a great rock in a weary land" (Isaiah 32:2).

I remember when we were working among the Indians, a little group of us had gone into an Indian village to present the Word. When we were on our way back to another village, we were overtaken by a tremendous thunder storm. We were near a great, overhanging cliff with a cave within, and our Indian guide led the way hastily through the pouring rain to this great rock, rising up from the floor of the desert, and in that cave we all found shelter. There were nearly thirty of us, and we stood looking out as the lightning flashed, and the water poured down all about us. There together we sang the hymn, "Rock of Ages." We were safe in the rock.

Oh, David knew something of the meaning of this, "Thou art my hiding place." ———

Playing Big Bear

My eldest son taught me a lesson along this line when he was just a little fellow. There was nothing he liked to play more than bear. First, we had to put some chairs in one corner of the room, with an opening between them. That was the bear's den. Then I had to get down on all fours, with a big shaggy overcoat over me and be the bear. The little fellow would walk past the den, trying to look as if he had no idea that a bear was anywhere near, when suddenly the savage beast would take after him, and we would run through one room and into another. The little fellow was pretty fleet on his feet, but, of course, he would always be caught at last.

The last time we ever played bear, he had run right into the corner of the kitchen, but the corner didn't open. He had his face right in the corner, and was so excited, that he just screamed. Suddenly, you know, the bear was about to spring, when the little fellow wheeled right about face, caught his breath, and said, "I am not a bit afraid. You are not a bear; you are just my own dear papa," and he jumped right into my arms.

I got to my feet, held the little fellow close to me, and tried to quiet him. I said to myself as I walked up and down with him, "Blessed God, it was just like this with me once. I was running away from Thee. I was afraid of Thee. I thought you wanted to destroy me. I tried to find a hiding place from Thee, but Thou didst never give me up."

I remembered the time years before when God ran me into a corner, and I couldn't get away; and instead of trying to run, I turned to Him in repentance, in confession, and said, "I am not afraid of Thee. Thou art not my enemy. I throw myself into Thy loving arms. Thou art my refuge. In Thy tender care and loving mercy, I find a hiding place."

> "Rock of Ages, cleft for me,
> Let me hide myself in Thee;
> Let the water and the blood,
> From Thy riven side which flowed,
> Be of sin the double cure,
> Save me from its guilt and power.

> "Not the labor of my hands
> Can fulfill Thy law's demands;
> Could my zeal no respite know,
> Could my tears forever flow.
> All for sin could not atone;
> Thou must save, and Thou alone."

Have you come to Him like that? Have you realized something of your own helplessness? Have you realized your own sinfulness, the utter hopelessness of your ever making atonement for your own guilt? Have you turned to Him as David, and said, "I will confess my transgressions unto the Lord." Then you have a right to add, "Thou forgavest the iniquity of my sin." He says, "For this shall every one that is godly pray unto thee in a time when thou mayest be found."

Prayer in the Wrong Place

Sometimes people put prayer in the wrong place. They have an idea that it is necessary to come to God and plead with Him, and pray to Him to put away their sins, and save them in His mercy. Dear friends, Scripture turns things just the other way. Paul says, "As though God did beseech you by us, we pray you in Christ's behalf, be ye reconciled to God."

I can remember the night I was converted. I can recall, though I was just fourteen, kneeling in my own room in the presence of God. I began to beseech Him to look upon me in grace, and save my soul. Then I thought, "What is it that I am asking God to do? I am asking Him to do something that He has been offering to do for years, but I have been refusing to permit Him to do it. I am asking Him to give me something—salvation, eternal life—which He has been offering me for years past, and yet here I come pleading for it. Why not simply accept His salvation and thank Him?"

I remember the words that came home to my soul, "He that believeth on him is not condemned; but he that believeth not is condemned already, because he hath not believed on the name of the only begotten Son of God." Kneeling there I said to Him, "Blessed God, I do believe in Thy Son. I trust Him now as my Saviour, and Thou hast told me, 'He that believeth on him is not condemned'." I knew then and there that He had saved me in His infinite love and kindness. I knew something of the meaning of David's expression, "Blessed is he whose transgression is forgiven, whose sin is covered."

If you are thinking seriously of these things, but do not know that your sins are forgiven, are covered, or that your soul is saved, let me say to you, just look up by faith to the Lord Jesus Christ, and He will save you right now. "He that believeth on him is not condemned; but he that believeth not is condemned already, because he hath not believed in the name of the only begotten Son of God."

CHAPTER VIII

THE GREATEST TEXT IN THE BIBLE

"For God so loved the world, that he gave his only begotten Son, that whosoever believeth in him should not
perish, but have everlasting life" (John 3:16).

WHY do so many people think this is the greatest text
in the Bible? There are other wonderful texts that
dwell on the love of God, that show how men are
delivered from judgment, that tell us how we may obtain
everlasting life, but no other one verse, as far as I can see,
gives us all these precious truths so clearly and so distinctly.
So true is this that when the gospel is carried into heathen
lands, and missionaries want to give a synopsis of the gospel
to a pagan people, all they find it necessary to do, if they are
going to a people that have a written language, is to trans-
late and print this verse, and it tells out the story that they
are so anxious for the people to hear. If they do not have
a written language, invariably one of the first scriptures that
they are taught to memorize is John 3:16.

I have a slip of paper sent to me by my friend, Allan Cameron of China. In those odd characters this same message
is written, and that message put into the hands of the
Chinese has often been used to lead a soul to Christ. Not
immediately, of course, for he does not understand it all at
once, but it has led him to ask upon what authority is this
statement based, and so eventually he is led to the Lord Jesus
Christ.

Many Truths in One Verse

How many truths are wrapped up in that one verse! In
the first place, there is the *personality of God*—"God so

loved." A God who can love is a person. We had a woman in the United States who invented a religion a few years ago, and she said it was all love, and yet she said that God is impersonal. But that is not possible. Just imagine falling in love with a cloud, or thinking that a cloud is loving you! It is something utterly impossible; you cannot do it. Behind love there must be a person with a warm, loving heart. *"God so loved."*

This Chinese translation which my friend Cameron sent me, says, "God so *passionately* loved the world, that he gave." It was a divine passion, a heart in heaven throbbing in loving sympathy with men in all their trials and difficulties here on earth. What a wonderful revelation that is, and it is all wrapped up in this one verse.

Then there is the truth of the *divine Fatherhood*. This God so loved men "that he gave his only begotten Son." There cannot be a son without a father. If God gave His Son, God Himself is a Father, and that is a revelation the pagan world never dreamed of.

Then again, there is the *lost condition of mankind*. God gave His well beloved Son, "that whosoever believeth in him should not perish, but have everlasting life." An unsaved man is in grave danger. You, dear unsaved one, are in grave danger of being so utterly lost that you may be banished from the presence of this God of love forever, and yet He it is who has provided a means whereby His banished ones may return to Him. God gave Him up to a sacrificial death on Calvary's cross for all men, "that whosoever believeth in him should not perish, but have everlasting life."

The *universality* of the offer of mercy is also here. It is a "whosoever" message, and what does *"whosoever"* mean? A gentleman came one time to my former home city and took an entire week for a series of lectures on John 3:16. During that time he labored every night to prove that the world that God loved was the world of the elect, and that *"whoso-ever"* was simply the "whosoever" that God had chosen from the foundation of the world. No wonder it took him a week to try to make out that kind of a thing. Any child can see the difference between a doctrine like that and that which is revealed in this text. Any one of school age knows the meaning of *"whosoever."*

You may have heard the story of the old Scotchman who had been brought up with the idea that God had predeter-mined just so many people to be saved, and all the rest were created to be damned. He felt that he ought to be willing to say, "O God, if it is Thy will to damn me, I do not want to be saved"; but he did want to be saved, and was in the deep-est agony of soul about it. But still they all said, "If you are not one of the elect, you cannot be saved."

One day he was out in the field plowing, when he found a piece of paper with a large text on it. He tried to spell it out, but he was not very good at reading, and so he read s l o w l y : "For—God—so—loved—the—world—that—he—gave—his—only—be-got-ten—Son—that—*who-so-ever.*" He wondered what that meant, but as he did not know, he passed on to the next part. "That—who-so-ever—be-liev-eth—in—him—should—not—perish—but—have—ever-last-ing—life."

"Man!" he said, "here's good news for somebody. God so loved the world, that he gave his only begotten Son, that *who-so-ever!* I wonder who is meant by that word. Here is somebody who can have everlasting life, elect or not elect." And while he was pondering the question, he saw a lad go-ing by with a bunch of books under his arm. He called to him, "Here, laddie, can ye read?"

"Aye, that I can," he replied.

"Well, will you read this?"

Wanting to impress the old man with his great ability, the boy read like a race horse; "For God so loved the world, that he gave his only begotten Son, that whosoever believeth in him should not perish, but have everlasting life."

"O laddie, laddie, don't read it so fast; read it again, and read it slowly so I can get every word, and be careful with that long word," said the old man. And so the boy read it again.

"Does it really say there that somebody can be saved by just believing?" the old man asked. "What does that long word mean?"

"Oh," said the boy, *"whosoever* means you, or me, or any other body; but there goes the bell, I have to run," and away he went.

The old man stood there, and read it again, "For God so loved the world, that he gave his only begotten Son, that you, or me, or any other body believeth in him, should not perish, but have everlasting life."

"Man!" he said, "that's good news for a sinner like me; I don't need to find out whether I am elect or not," and he dropped down between the plow handles, and there confessed himself a sinner for whom Jesus died. He took God at His word and his soul was saved.

One Text a Whole Week

One of the earliest stories I ever heard about D. L. Moody was one with which some of you are familiar. When he was in Great Britain, he met a young Englishman by the name of Henry Moorhouse. One day Moorhouse said to Moody, "I am thinking of going to America."

"Well," said Moody, "if you should ever be in Chicago, come down to my place, and I will give you a chance to preach."

Now although Mr. Moody was not two-faced, he was merely trying to be polite, for mentally he was saying, "I hope he won't come." There are so many people, you know, who want to preach, although God never meant them to, and Mr. Moody was not quite sure of Mr. Moorhouse. He was rather taken back one day when, just before leaving for a series of meetings, he received a telegram, "Have just arrived in New York. Will be in Chicago on Sunday."

"And now," thought Moody, "I am going away, and I told him he could preach here." So he said to his wife and to his committee, "Here's this young Englishman coming; let him preach once, and then if the people enjoy him, put him on again."

When Moody returned, he said to his wife, "Well, what about that young preacher?"

"Oh," she said, "he is a better preacher than you are, Why, he is telling sinners that God loves them."

"He is wrong!" said Moody, "God doesn't love sinners."

"Well," she said, "you go and hear him."

"Why, is he still preaching?" asked Mr. Moody.

"Yes, he has been preaching all week and has taken only one text, John 3:16," was her reply.

When Mr. Moody went to the meeting, Moorhouse got up, and said, "I have been hunting and hunting all through the Bible, looking for a text, and I think we will just talk about John 3:16 once more." Mr. Moody always testified that it was on that night that he got his first clear understanding of the gospel and the love of God. Think what it meant in Moody's life, and in the lives of tens of thousands who were reached through his ministry, to know that God loves sinners. Are you one of those who has been saying, "If I were only a little better, I could believe that God loves me?" O dear friend, hear it again:

> "Sinners Jesus will receive;
> Sound this word of grace to all
> Who the heavenly pathway leave,
> All who linger, all who fall."

"This is a faithful saying, and worthy of all acceptation, that Christ Jesus came into the world to save sinners; of whom I am chief" (1 Timothy 1:15).

Just Like African Boys

I remember when I was a boy, going to a missionary meeting. A missionary was there from Africa, and was showing us a whole lot of curious things, and then he said, "Now boys, I want to tell you the kind of gospel we preach to the people in Africa. How many good boys have we here?" A lot of us thought we were good, but our mothers were there, and so not one of us dared hold up his hand. "Well," said he, "not one good boy here; then I have the same message for you that we have for the heathen in Africa; God loves naughty boys!"

"My," I thought, "he is getting all mixed up," for you see I had heard people say, "If you are good, God will love you." But, dear friends, that is not true. God is not waiting for you to be good so He can love you; God loves sinners, and has proven His love for them by the gift of His Son, the Lord Jesus Christ. "Herein is love, not that we loved God, but that he loved us, and sent his Son to be the propitiation for our sins" (1 John 4:10). Instead of waiting for people to be good, "God commendeth his love toward us, in that, while we were yet sinners, Christ died for us" (Romans 5:8). Do you believe it, dear friend?

The difficulty is that men have this wrong idea about God, and are always trying to make out that they are better than they are. "Most men will proclaim every one his own goodness: but a faithful man who can find?" (Proverbs 20:6). You will find people down in the depths of sin, but they are always ready to compare themselves with other folk, saying, "I am as good as they are." But God has no message and no blessing for men who are trying to justify themselves.

As long as you try to make a good name for yourself, God can only condemn you; but when you come into His presence and confess yourself a lost, guilty sinner, God has a message and a blessing for you. "God so loved the world"—a wicked, corrupt, and ungodly world, and you and I belong to it. "As in water face answereth to face, so the heart of man to man" (Proverbs 27:19). God's Word declares that "The heart is deceitful above all things, and desperately wicked: who can know it? I the Lord search the heart, I try the reins, even to give every man according to his ways, and according to the fruit of his doings" (Jeremiah 17:9, 10). Yet, knowing all the wickedness of which my heart and your heart is capable, God loves us and gave His Son to die for us.

My! what a gospel this is; what a message to bring to poor, needy sinners! We do not come to men, and say, "Turn over a new leaf; quit your meanness; give up this, and give up that." We do not ask any one to *give up;* we ask you to *receive* the gift of God, and when you receive that gift, "the things of the world will grow strangely dim in the light of Christ's glory and grace."

A lad tried to preach on John 3:16 one day. He was asked to give his testimony, but thought he had better get up a sermon. He divided his text into four heads:

1. God loved.
2. God gave.
3. I believe.
4. I have.

Could you make a better division than that?

A Girl's Horror of God

A little girl who lived in Luther's day had been brought up with a perfect horror of God. She thought of Him as always watching her, taking note of every wrong thing she did, and just waiting to visit judgment upon her. Her parents could not get that fear out of her mind. Her father was a printer, and was working on Luther's first German Bible. One day she was in his shop, when just a corner of one of the sheets of the Bible caught her eye. She looked at it, and as she read it, her whole attitude toward God changed, and she said, "Mother, I am not afraid of God any more."

"Well, my dear," said the mother, "I am glad of that, but why are you not afraid of God?"

"Oh," she replied, "look what I found, a piece of the Bible, and it says, 'God so loved, that he gave.'" It was just a part of two lines.

"Well," her mother said, "how does that take away your fear of God? It doesn't say what He gave."

"Oh, but if He loved us enough to give anything, I am not afraid," said the child. And then her mother sat down and opened up the whole truth to her.

People are stumbling over the simplest things. Take, for instance, that word *believeth.* You would think that was plain enough for anybody, but all my life I have heard people say, "I have always believed, and yet I am not saved." It does not say, "Whosoever believeth the *Bible,* or *creeds,* or even the *gospel story,*" but it does say, "Whosoever believeth in *him.*"

What is it to believe in Him? It means to put your soul's confidence in Him, to trust in Him, God's blessed Son. When in Toronto, I picked up a copy of a broad Scotch translation of the New Testament, and the first thing I noticed was that this word *believeth* is not found there at all. Instead of *believeth* there is the Scotch word, *lippen,* and it means *to throw your whole weight upon.* This is the way it reads, "Whosoever lippens to Jesus should not perish, but have the life of the ages"—the life that runs on through all the ages.

Just Lippen to Jesus

One day Dr. Chalmers spent hours with a poor, anxious soul, trying to lead her into peace, but she could not understand what it was to believe, and finally he had to leave her. On the way home he had to cross a creek with a shaky old bridge over it, and as he was feeling his way across in a very careful manner, one of his parishioners who saw him, called out, "Can you nae lippen the bridge?" Immediately he said, "That's the word for the old lady I have just left," and he went back to her, and said, "I have got the word for you, can you nae *lippen* to Jesus?"

"Lippen?" she said, "is it just to lippen? Aye, I can lippen to Him. He will never let me down, will He?"

"Yes, that is it," he replied, "He will never let you down."

Have you been struggling, trying, working; have you been promising and trying to give up this and to do this, that, and the other thing? O dear friend, hear it, "Whosoever *lippens* to Jesus shall not perish, but have everlasting life."

Another "Whosoever"

But now notice the alternative. They who trust in Jesus will not perish, but what about those who do not trust in Him? There is another *whosoever*. In Revelation 20, where we have that solemn picture of the last judgment, we read, "I saw a great white throne, and him that sat on it, from whose face the earth and the heaven fled away; and there was found no place for them. And I saw the dead, small and great, stand before God; and the books were opened: and another book was opened, which is the book of life: and the dead were judged out of those things which were written in the books, according to their works. And the sea gave up the dead which were in it; and death and hell delivered up the dead which were in them: and they were judged every man according to their works. And death and hell were cast into the lake of fire. This is the second death. And *whosoever* was not found written in the book of life was cast into the lake of fire" (Revelation 20:11-15).

Listen to it, sinner, *whosoever* in the day of judgment "was not found written in the book of life was cast into the lake of fire." Who are found written in the book of life? *"Whosoever* believeth in him should not perish, but have everlasting life." There they are, those who believed, and those that did not believe; those who received the gift of God, and those who spurned the gospel, trampling under foot the grace of God. They stand in the judgment as poor, lost, trembling souls to hear their dreadful sentence. You may be saved now without money and without price.

> "There is life for a look at the Crucified One,
>   There is life at this moment for thee;
> Then look, sinner, look unto Him and be saved,
>   Unto Him who was nailed to the tree."

Look, sinner, look to Jesus just now and be saved.

CHAPTER IX

HOW TO BECOME A CHILD OF GOD

"He came unto his own, and his own received him not. But as many as received him, to them gave he power to become the sons of God, even to them that believe on his name: which were born, not of blood, nor of the will of the flesh, nor of the will of man, but of God" (John 1:11-13).

HOW does a man become a Christian? The verses of the text, I believe, answer the question, and they do so first negatively and then positively. There are three ways indicated by which one cannot become a child of God, and only one way by which he can. Look at verse 13, "Which were born, not of blood, nor of the will of the flesh, nor of the will of man."

Not of Blood

Observe, it is not of *blood*. You may inherit a great many natural characteristics from your parents that men may admire; you may inherit tastes, features, and dispositions in some measure at least, but you cannot inherit the grace of God. It is just as true of the children of Christian parents, as it is of any other people born into this world, that they must be born again.

I remember a few years ago my wife and I and our children were on our way West. We were passing through Colorado. My eldest son, who was just a little boy at the time, was fond of going through the train, playing that he was the news agent. He said, "Father, have you any tracts I could give out?" I had some, and so handed them to him. They sometimes stop me when I go through the train giving out tracts, but I thought they would not stop the little fellow. He handed everybody one of these gospel tracts, and soon most of the people were reading them. A little later I was passing through the car and a lady occupying one of the sections stopped me, and said, "I beg your pardon, sir, but I think it was your child who gave me this tract, was it not?"

"Yes," I said, "it was."

"Won't you sit down a moment?" she asked.

So I introduced my wife, and we sat down.

"You cannot imagine," she said, "how pleased I am to know that there are other religious people on this train."

"You are interested in these things?" I inquired.

"Yes indeed," she said, "I have been religious all my life."

"When were you born again?" I asked.

"Oh," she replied, "my father was a class-leader, and an uncle and two brothers of mine are all clergymen."

"That is very interesting," I said, "and may I ask again, have you been converted yourself?"

"Why, you don't seem to understand; my father was a class-leader, and my uncle and two brothers are earnest clergymen."

"But you don't expect to go to heaven hanging on their coat-tails, even if they are born again, do you? Have you been truly converted to God yourself?" I asked.

"Not at all," she replied, "but I thought if I put it that way you would understand that religion runs in our family."

"Religion may run in your family, but religion and Christianity are two very different things," I said. "There are a great many people who are intensely religious, but they are not saved. Our blessed Lord was speaking to a very religious man when he said, 'Ye must be born again.'"

I had great difficulty getting that lady to see that salvation is not of blood. She could scarcely understand how a family such as hers needed regeneration. Perhaps you have rather prided yourself in the fact that you too came from a line of Christian progenitors, and have taken it for granted that because your parents were Christians, you are. "Which were born, *not* of blood." You are not a Christian simply because you were born into a Christian family.

Not of the Will of the Flesh

Then we read, "Nor of the *will of the flesh.*" What does that mean? It just means that you cannot make yourself a Christian by any self-determination. Suppose that you said to yourself, "I have made up my mind that from tonight on I am going to be a Christian," that would not make you one. It is very good to come to a decision like that, to come to the place where you make up your mind to become a Christian, but that will not make you a child of God. If I were born in some country where they have a hereditary monarchy, I might say, "I am tired of being just one of the commonalty; I have made up my mind that from now on I am going to be a member of the royal family." I might go to a tailor, show him a picture of a royal person, and say to him, "Now, dress me up like that." And I might begin to sign myself as a royal highness, or some other high-sounding title, but I would only be a fraud, for no man ever became a member of the royal family by the will of the flesh; he has to be born into the family.

No one ever became a child of God by simply making up his mind that he would be a Christian. You could do that according to your own standards, if Jesus had never died on the cross. You could make up your mind that from a given time you would call yourself a child of God, try to live as a child of God should live, even though Jesus had never suffered and bled and died for your sins upon the tree. Why did He go to the cross, if simply by an act of your will, you could make yourself a Christian?

You have no more power to make yourself a Christian than I have to make myself the president of the United States. If I should go into politics, no matter how favorably the people might look upon me, nor how able I might be, I could never become president of the United States, because I was born on the other side of the line. I was born in Toronto, Canada, and the Constitution of the United States says that no man can be president who was not born in this country. I might make up my mind to become a politician, and do my best to ingratiate myself with the people, but I never could become president of the United States, because although I am a naturalized citizen, I was born an alien. No man can ever become a child of God by making up his mind to be a Christian. You have to be born a child of God, and it is too late to be born that way the first time; but thank God, you can be born again.

Not of Man

In the third place, we read, "Which were born, not of blood, nor of the will of the flesh, nor of the *will of man.*" From the humblest clergyman up to the pope of Rome, or, if you want to turn it around the other way, from the pope up to a Protestant parson, there is no man on earth so holy and so closely in touch with God that he can make a Christian of you by anything he can do for you. He might baptize you, he might confirm you, he might recommend that you be received into church membership, but he could not make a Christian of you by voting you into the membership of the church. If you came in without being born again, you would be just a poor lost sinner with a false profession.

I remember some years ago when that mighty man of God, Henry Varley, was in California having meetings in a large church. One night he said to me, "I want you to come downstairs with me; they are going to have a church meeting, and they have some applicants for membership. I would like to get a line on them, see how careful they are about receiving people, for this will help me to know how to preach." There were four candidates for membership. The minister said, "We are glad to have our brethren here to apply for membership in this church, and we want them to give us a word, and then they will be voted on."

The first man stood to his feet, and said something like this: "My friends, you all know me; my father and mother have been members of this church for years. I have often felt I should join the church, and so I made up my mind that if you would accept me, I would like to feel that I am a member of the church of my parents."

A gentleman spoke up, and said, "May I ask the young man a question?" and the minister said, "Well, if it is a proper one, you may."

"I would like to ask if you have ever been born again."

The minister jumped to his feet, and said, "I object; I do not want our brother to attempt to answer that question. That is downright impertinence; that matter is entirely between the individual and his God."

And so they voted him in; but I remembered that my Bible said, "Not of blood."

The second young man stood to his feet, and spoke somewhat as follows: "Well, friends, you know me. I haven't always been what I ought to be, but last New Year I made up my mind to turn over a new leaf, and try to do better. I think it would help me to join the church, and so I have applied for membership." And they voted him in.

My friend had found it did not pay to ask questions, so did not try it again. I remembered then that my Bible said, "Nor of the will of the flesh."

The third young man arose, and with choice English accent said, "You know, my friends, I haven't been in the habit of attending a church of this nomenclature. Over in England I attended the state church. When I was a little child, I was baptized by the Archbishop of Canterbury. But since coming to America, I have enjoyed coming down here, and thought I would like to join with you." So they voted him in.

But I remembered again that my Bible said, "Nor of the will of man."

There were the three of them. One of them thought he was a Christian because his parents were, the second because he had turned over a new leaf, and the third because he had been baptized by a great church dignitary.

There was one other man sitting there, older than these others, and I could see the marks which sin had left upon his brow. When he was introduced, he spoke with great fervency: "My friends, I do not need to say very much; you know my story. My dear wife and children have been members with you here for a number of years. You know what a life I have led; I have been a drunkard, a poor sinner; I alienated my wife and children from me so that they had to leave me. I was going down, down, down in my sins, and it seemed there was no power to stop me. About six months ago, I made up my mind there was no help for me, and started down Market Street toward the water front, intending to jump in and end it all; but as I got to Seventh and Market, the Salvation Army were having an open air meeting. I went over and they were singing of the cleansing power of the blood of Christ."

> "Oh! precious is the flow
> That makes me white as snow;
> No other fount I know,
>   Nothing but the blood of Jesus."

"I listened! They sang it over and over, until they sang the words right into my soul, and I said: 'I wonder if it is true, if there is hope for a sinner like me'; and then I listened to one and another tell how they too had been lost in sin, and Jesus had saved them, and when someone invited any poor sinner to come and kneel with them at the old drum, I threw myself down, and cried, 'O God, if there is hope for a sinner like me, save me tonight.' Something happened that night; I trusted Christ; He took me in; He made me a new creature; I was born of God; and all has been different ever since; we have a happy home now"—and then he burst into tears. Well, they voted him in, but I could not help but wonder why he wanted to get into an ice-box like that.

There you have three ways by which you cannot become a child of God, and there is the way and the only way, by which you can become a child of God. This getting converted is a divine thing; it is a divine work—something that the Spirit of God does for the poor sinner who comes to Christ. How is it all brought about?

The One Divine Way

"He came unto his own, and his own received him not. But as many as received him, to them gave he power to become the sons of God, even to them that believe on his name." You see that is very different from simply making a lip confession of Christianity; that is a very different thing from turning over a new leaf, joining a church, being baptized, or something like that. *"As many as received him"* means just this, that the poor sinner comes to the place where he gives up all hope of saving himself, and says, "O Christ, come in and dwell with me alone." No one ever invited Him to enter who was disappointed. "Behold, I stand at the door and knock: if any man hear my voice, and open the door, I will come in to him, and will sup with him, and he with me."

Is your heart's door bolted against Him? Have you lived up to the present moment with Christ outside? Will you open the door?

You say, "How can I receive Him? I cannot see Him. In what way can I receive Him?"

"As many as received him, to them gave he power to become the sons of God, even to them that believe on his name." Do you believe on His name? What does it mean to believe on His name? It means to put your trust in Him. His name speaks of all that He is. "Thou shalt call his name Jesus: for he shall save his people from their sins" (Matthew 1:21). John Hambleton used to say, "There are just five letters to our English word, *Jesus,* and they mean just this: *Jesus Exactly Suits Us Sinners.*" We are poor, lost, guilty men and women, but He is the holy One, God's blessed Son, and He went to Calvary's cross and died for us, bore our sins in His own body on the tree, and now God says, "Will you receive my Son? Will you trust Him? Will you believe on His name?" If you will, He will save your precious soul, and will give you the right to call yourself a child of God. No one has that right unless he is born again. Peter says, "Being born again, not of corruptible seed, but of incorruptible, by the word of God, which liveth and abideth forever. . . . And this is the word which by the gospel is preached unto you." (1 Peter 1:23, 25).

What is it then that you need to believe in order to be saved? "Repent ye, and believe the gospel" (Mark 1:15). What is the gospel? It is God's "good news" about His blessed Son. He tells us that "Christ died for our sins according to the scriptures; and that he was buried, and that he rose again the third day according to the scriptures" (1 Corinthians 15:3, 4). And again: "If thou shalt confess with thy mouth the Lord Jesus, and shalt believe in thine heart that God hath raised him from the dead, thou shalt be saved. For with the heart man believeth unto righteousness; and with the mouth confession is made unto salvation" (Romans 10:9, 10).

The sinner who addresses you was once hurrying down in his sins to a lost eternity, but when Jesus called, he came to Him, put his trust in Him, and He saved his soul forty years ago. He is waiting now to save you. There is no reason why you should go on longer without settling this vital matter. When I write to you about being saved by believing, I do not mean that you are simply to credit the gospel story in an intellectual kind of way, and go right on in the same life; but if you realize you are a lost sinner, and want to be saved from the guilt and power of your sins, I beseech you to yield to His entreaty, and put your trust in the One who died for you. God will work the miracle of regeneration in your soul, and you will know that you are born again. "Which were born, not of blood, nor of the will of the flesh, nor of the will of man, but of God."

CHAPTER X

ANATHEMA MARANATHA

"If any man love not the Lord Jesus Christ, let him be Anathema Maranatha" (1 Corinthians 16:22).

THIS is one of the most incisive and challenging statements in all the Bible. Incisive because there is no possibility of misunderstanding it. In the fewest possible words, it declares the inevitable doom of all who do not love the Lord Jesus.

Challenging, first because of its very incisiveness; and second, because of the fact that it contains two untranslated foreign words, Anathema Maranatha, taken from two different languages, and which by their very strangeness compel our attention.

Anathema is Greek and means "accursed," or "devoted to judgment." It is the same word that the apostle uses in Galatians 1:8, 9: "But though we, or an angel from heaven, preach any other gospel unto you than that which we have preached unto you, let him be accursed. As we said before, so say I now again, If any man preach any other gospel unto you than that ye have received, let him be accursed." The man or angel who misleads others with a false gospel is under the ban of the Eternal God;—Anathema, "accursed," "devoted to judgment." He uses the same word again when speaking of himself: he says, "I could wish that myself were accursed, (Anathema, R.V.) from Christ for my brethren, my kinsmen according to the flesh." It implies then clearly a definite separation from Christ, banishment from God, without any hope of restoration.

Then the other word, "Maranatha," is a compound word,

an Aramaic expression of Chaldean origin, translated "our
Lord come!" or "the Lord cometh!" It is a vivid reminder
that the rejected Christ is to return in glory as Judge of the
living and the dead.

So then the strange compound expression, this Greco—
Aramaic term, "Anathema Maranatha," might really be rendered, "devoted to judgment; our Lord cometh." Slightly
paraphrasing the entire sentence, it would read, "If any man
love not our Lord Jesus Christ, he will be devoted to judgment at the coming of the Lord." What a tremendously solemn statement and how seriously we should consider it!

Notice that according to this passage unless you are a
lover of Christ, unless He is precious to you, you are not
really saved; and if you are unregenerated, you do not love
Him.   More than that, you cannot love Him even if you
try.   It is not in your power to make yourself love Him. You
do not have in your heart one atom of love for Christ in
your natural condition.   And yet if you do not love Him,
you must be accursed at His coming.   Could anything be
more solemn?

The Human Heart

Our Lord Himself sounded all the depths of the human
heart, the heart which is "deceitful above all things, and desperately wicked," which God alone really knows.   He tells
what He found in it, what proceeds out of it, and there is no
hint of anything good; no righteousness, no holiness, no
love.   You cannot get good things out of the natural heart
because they are not there.   Hear what He, who spake as
"never man spake," has said concerning this: "But those
things which proceed out of the mouth come forth from the
heart; and they defile the man.   For out of the heart proceed
evil thoughts, murders, adulteries, fornications, thefts, false
witness, blasphemies: these are the things which defile a man:

but to eat with unwashen hands defileth not a man" (Matthew 15:18-20).

Then again in Galatians 5:19-21, the Holy Spirit gives us a long list of the works of the flesh, but you search the record in vain to find anything about love or goodness. Listen to the appalling list: "Now the works of the flesh are manifest, which are these; Adultery, fornication, uncleanness, lasciviousness, idolatry, witchcraft, hatred, variance, emulations, wrath, strife, seditions, heresies, envyings, murders, drunkenness, revellings, and such like: of the which I tell you before, as I have also told you in time past, that they which do such things shall not inherit the kingdom of God."

This is what you and I are capable of by nature. These are the things that abound in our hearts. Decency may keep us from following out all our evil inclinations, but these are the sins to which we are liable, one person just as much as another, if exposed to temptation. It is written: "As in water face answereth to face, so the heart of man to man." And again, "There is no difference, for all have sinned, and come short of the glory of God."

If then the great test of salvation is love for the Lord Jesus Christ, and you do not possess that love, you are lost, no matter how respectable your outward life may be. And if you say to yourself, "From now on I am going to love Him; I refuse to spurn Him; I will make myself devoted to Him," let me warn you not to try, for your efforts will end in disappointment and despair. You do not love the Lord Jesus Christ if unregenerated, and you cannot love Him unless God Himself produces that love within your soul.

By this we see the absolute necessity of a second birth. Now, indeed, we understand why it is that "except a man be born again, he cannot see the kingdom of God. That which is born of the flesh is flesh," and there is no possible way by which it can be changed into spirit. The works of the flesh are unholy; the will of the flesh is ever opposed to the will of God. "The carnal mind," which is the mind of the flesh, "is not subject to the law of God, neither indeed can be." Hence man as born after the flesh is hopelessly lost, unless God intervenes.

But blessed be His Name, that "which is born of the Spirit is spirit." It is possible for man, totally depraved though he is by nature, to be regenerated by divine power, born again by the Word of God and the Spirit of God, and so become a new creature in Christ Jesus, producing fruit for God.

Man Totally Depraved

Some of you may object to that old theological term, "total depravity." You do not like to think of yourself as quite so far gone. But I beg you to remember that man as created by God is tripartite—spirit, and soul, and body. If in every part, man has been affected by the fall, then he has become totally affected, and inasmuch as he has been affected not for good, but for evil, he is totally depraved.

Your body is depraved. No man possesses today the splendid physique that our first parents possessed from the moment of their creation. Your body is subject to all kinds of ills, sickness, weakness, pain, and death. And moreover, everyone of your natural appetites or propensities is depraved. There is not one of them that is today functioning exactly as originally intended. "God hath made man upright, but they have sought out many inventions." Every physical appetite is capable of perversion, and with this perversion comes sure and certain ill effects, all the result of sin: "Receiving in themselves that recompense of their error which was meet" (Romans 1:27).

Your soul is depraved. The soul, according to Scripture, is the seat of your entire emotional nature. But what man would dare to say that his emotions are all under divine control? He cannot trust himself when under the power of strong emotion even for one moment. Your very affections can no longer be depended upon. You wound and injure the very ones you profess to love the most. How true the words of that wretched man, who himself was one of the most striking illustrations of the very fact I am stressing, Oscar Wilde, who wrote, "Each man kills the thing he loves." I venture to say that if you were to follow your natural affections and the desires of your emotional nature to the limit, your whole life would be wrecked and ruined.

Your spirit is depraved. The spirit is the highest part of man, that which distinguishes him from the brute creation; that which gives him the ability to form judgments, and above all else to hear the voice of God speaking to him. "The spirit of man is the candle of the Lord, searching the inmost parts of his being." But what man is constantly obeying the voice of the Lord? Have we not all turned away from Him in our pride and our folly, preferring our own will to the will of God? "The lusts of the mind" are as vile in His sight as "the lusts of the flesh."

And yet it is to such men that the Spirit of God says, "If any man love not our Lord Jesus Christ, let him be Anathema Maranatha"—devoted to judgment at the Lord's return! How solemnly this reveals our true condition, and how it ought to stir our hearts, and lead us to cry to God to do for us that which we cannot do for ourselves; to create in us a clean heart; to implant His divine love; to subdue these stubborn wills of ours; and to claim us for Himself.

And this is exactly what He offers to do in the gospel. In order that He might effect this change in us, that He might impart to us a new life, the very nature of which is love, the Lord Jesus Christ went to the cross and there tasted death for us. The only way whereby we can begin to love

Him is by believing the gospel message, and trusting Him as our personal Saviour. It is when I learn that "the Son of God loved me, and gave himself for me," that my heart cries out, "We love him, because he first loved us." Oh, I beg of you take time today to stand in faith at the foot of Calvary's cross! By the aid of the Word of God which so clearly depicts that awful scene, fix your eyes upon the wounded, bleeding Sufferer, the thorn-crowned Saviour, hanging there upon the nails for you. Listen to His tender pleading: "Father, forgive them, for they know not what they do." Hear His cry of anguish as He took the lost sinner's place, and bore the lost sinner's judgment, "My God, my God, why hast Thou forsaken me?" and say to yourself over and over until you believe it with all your heart: "It was all for me; He died that I might live; He loved me even unto death." As you thus put your heart's trust in Him, and believe in Him as your own personal Saviour, you will find He imparts a new nature, and this nature manifests itself in love. You will love Him, and you will love His people, because the love of God will be shed abroad in your heart by the Holy Ghost given unto you.

See how this blessed truth is illustrated in the history of John Newton. He was a blackbirder, slave trader, drunkard, utterly godless, and lost to all decency until, broken down by grace divine, he gazed by faith upon the suffering Saviour. Hear him sing:

"In evil long I took delight,
   Unawed by shame or fear;
Till a new Object met my sight
   And stopped my wild career.

"I saw One hanging on a tree,
   In agony and blood;
He fixed His dying eyes on me,
   As near His cross I stood.

"Sure never till my latest breath,
  Can I forget that look;
It seemed to charge me with His death,
  Though not a word He spoke.

"My conscience felt and owned my guilt,
  And plunged me in despair;
I saw my sins His blood had spilt,
  And helped to nail Him there.

"A second look He gave, which said,
  I freely all forgive;
This blood is for thy ransom paid;
  I die that thou may'st live."

And John Newton was a new man; the old vile life was ended forever, and from that hour he loved the Lord Jesus Christ above every earthly friend, above everything this world could offer. And so at last he could say:

"Then I, who trembling learned to see
  That I my Lord had slain,
Was filled with peace, because for me
  He bore that grief and pain.

"Thus while His death my sin displays
  In all its blackest hue;
Such is the mystery of grace,
  It seals my pardon too."

Oh, that every unsaved person might see what John Newton saw, might believe what John Newton believed, and then he too would love the Lord Jesus Christ, and be forever freed from the danger of judgment at His coming.

It is a common saying among men that "love begets love." Surely if this is ever true it ought to be true in connection with the love of God to mankind. We are told that "He so loved the world, that he gave his only begotten Son, that whosoever believeth in him should not perish, but have ever-lasting life." And again, "In this was manifested the love of God toward us, because that God sent his only begotten Son into the world, that we might live through him. Herein is love, not that we loved God, but that he loved us, and sent his Son to be the propitiation for our sins." Because we were dead in trespasses and in sins, the love of God caused Him to send His blessed Son, that in Him we might receive eternal life. Because we were guilty and deserving of His judgment, He sent His Son to be the propitiation, the atonement for our sins. It is as the Holy Spirit brings these truths to bear in power upon our souls that we become partakers of the divine nature, and we love Him who has so wondrously undertaken for us.

Apart from the manifestation of God in Christ, there is no revelation of divine love. We see the power and wisdom of God manifested in creation. In His provision for man's need and comfort, we have many evidences of His goodness, but His love is shown in the Cross. "God commendeth his love toward us, in that, while we were yet sinners, Christ died for us." Who can fathom the wickedness of the man who tramples such grace beneath his feet, and persists in sinning against love like this? Need we wonder that the Holy Spirit has said, "If any man love not the Lord Jesus Christ, let him be Anathema Maranatha" (devoted to judgment at the Lord's coming)?

Chapter XI

INSIDE THE VEIL AND OUTSIDE THE CAMP

"Having therefore, brethren, boldness to enter into the holiest by the blood of Jesus, by a new and living way, which he hath consecrated for us, through the veil, that is to say, his flesh; and having an high priest over the house of God; let us draw near with a true heart in full assurance of faith" (Hebrews 10:19-22).

"Wherefore Jesus also, that he might sanctify the people with his own blood, suffered without the gate. Let us go forth therefore unto him without the camp, bearing his reproach" (Hebrews 13:12,13).

THE Old Testament is a very wonderful picture book of New Testament truths. No uninspired writer has ever produced a volume of gospel illustrations that compares with the Old Testament in type, shadow, or symbol. All through the sacred pages of the earlier books we have set forth the wonderful truths that have been made known to us by our Lord Jesus Christ.

Those of you who are familiar with the Tabernacle will recall the place which the veil had in connection with its furnishings and ordinances. By it the sanctuary was divided into two parts; the first was called the Holy Place, and into that particular room the priests went ministering from day to day. In it there were three pieces of furniture—the golden candlestick, speaking of Christ as the light of the world; the golden table of shew bread, speaking of Christ as the One who maintains and sustains His people through their wilderness journey; and the altar of incense, which speaks of Christ ever living to make intercession for us.

Then there was the inner sanctuary on the other side of

the veil, called the Holiest of All, and in this room there was just one piece of furniture, the ark of the covenant, surmounted by the mercy seat. This was the dwelling place of God, and the mercy seat on top of the ark was the meeting place of God and man. An uncreated light, the Shekinah glory, shone above the mercy seat between the golden cherubim, whose wings were spread out over it. Into this sacred inclosure, where the presence of God was manifested, the ordinary priests were not permitted to enter; only the High Priest, and that just once a year. He went in carrying a golden basin filled with atoning blood, which he sprinkled upon the mercy seat and before it, where he himself took his stand.

This was God's figure for the time then present, we are told in the Epistle to the Hebrews, when no man could have immediate access to God. There was a priesthood provided through which people drew nigh unto God in a ritualistic way, but God commanded that the people should stand afar off to worship Him, and the man who drew near was put to death. The only exception was the High Priest once every year.

The Veil of Separation

The veil which hung between the Holy Place and the Most Holy was most significant, for we are told in Hebrews that it represented the flesh of our Lord Jesus Christ, that is, it represented Him as a man here on earth. The veil was composed of fine twined linen, ornamented with threads of blue and purple and scarlet, and cherubim were wrought upon it, setting forth the justice and judgment of God. The fine twined linen pictures, as it always does in Scripture, perfect righteousness, the spotless and righteous life of the Lord Jesus Christ, the sinless One, in whom is no sin, for He knew no sin. The blue suggested His heavenly character. He was not a mere man, born as other men are; He was the Son of man from heaven. The purple spoke of royal dignity. He was the Son of David, the Son of Abraham, the One who came to reign on earth, the righteous King.

The scarlet is most significant. It literally means, "The splendor of a worm." This seems a strange expression to us, but it need not be. In Mexico there is a little insect that feeds on cactus, called the cochineal. It is ground up in a mortar and its blood makes a crimson dye. Also in Palestine, there was a little worm called the tola. When it was crushed, it produced the scarlet dye which was used in making the beautiful garments that clothed the nobility. In Psalm 22:6, the Lord says, "I am a worm, and no man; a reproach of men, and despised of the people." He took the lowest place, the place of a worm, and was crushed in death that you and I might be clothed with the beautiful garments of right-eousness and glory. The scarlet speaks of suffering and of glory. Think, then, how wonderfully that veil sets forth the Lord Jesus Christ, the heavenly One, the kingly One, the suffering One, the righteous One.

The Way into the Holiest

But the unrent veil shut man out from God, and the holy spotless life of Jesus was in itself a barrier rather than a means of approach to God. The unrent flesh of Jesus only served to shut God in and to shut man out. Jesus said, "Except a corn of wheat fall into the ground and die, it abideth alone; but if it die, it bringeth forth much fruit" (John 12:24). Men seem to think that our blessed Lord came to earth as an example to show us what man ought to be or do in order to obtain God's favor. The life of our Lord, in-stead of being an example which unconverted men may fol-low in order that they might find their way into the pres-ence of God, is simply the condemnation of all men everywhere, for in Christ we see what man should be, but what no man ever was, "For all have sinned, and come short of the glory of God" (Romans 3:23).

The unrent flesh of Jesus was a barrier into the presence of God. No man is perfect as Jesus was, and therefore no man has a title as He had to enter into the presence of God uncondemned. But now the glorious gospel is this, that the holy One, the perfect One, the righteous One, the heavenly One, the kingly One, went to Calvary's cross, and there His flesh was rent; there He took the place of guilty sinners; there He was wounded for our transgressions, He was bruised for our iniquities, He, the sinless One, was made sin for us.

> "All our iniquities on Him were laid;
> All our indebtedness by Him was paid."

He took the sinner's place, and bore the sinner's judgment. He drank the cup of wrath that sinners so justly deserve to drink, endured the awful forsaking of God, and cried out at last, "My God, my God, why hast thou forsaken me?" Then, having drained that cup to the bitter dregs, having borne the judgment that you and I so richly deserve, He cried in triumph, ere He surrendered His spirit to the Father, "It is finished!"

When He died, we read that "the veil of the temple was rent in twain from the top to the bottom"; not from the bottom to the top as though some priest might have torn it asunder, but from the top to the bottom. It was the hand of God that rent that veil, in order to declare that now the way into His immediate presence has been opened through the rent flesh of His beloved Son. We read in the New Testament, "Having therefore, brethren, boldness to enter into the holiest by the blood of Jesus, by a new and living way, which he consecrated (or dedicated for us) through the veil, that is to say, his flesh" (Hebrews 10:19, 20).

"The Holiest we enter
In perfect peace with God,
Through whom we found our center
In Jesus and His blood.
Though great may be our dullness
In thought and word and deed,
We glory in the fullness
Of Him that meets our need.

"Much incense is ascending
Before th'eternal throne;
God graciously is bending
To hear each feeble groan.
To all our prayers and praises
Christ adds His sweet perfume,
And Love the censer raises
These odors to consume."

And there into the immediate presence of God, He who died upon the cross to put away our sins has entered as our great High Priest. We are told in Hebrews that He is entered within the veil as our forerunner. His place in the Holiest is the pledge that all who believe on Him shall be there. He has gone in as our representative. He has gone in to announce to God the Father that through the virtue of His shed blood untold millions shall also be there.

A Pilgrim Path

In the meantime, we are walking the sands of the desert. We are still down here on earth, and while we are here we have our trials, our sicknesses, our sufferings, and our sorrows to endure, but that loving heart of His feels for every one of His people in their trials and griefs, and presents the incense of His own constant intercession there in the presence of God on our behalf. We may well say:

> "O God, we come with singing,
>   Because Thy great High Priest
> Our names to Thee is bringing,
>   Nor e'er forgets the least.
>
> For us He wears the mitre,
>   Where 'Holiness' shines bright;
> For us His robes are whiter
>   Than heaven's unsullied light."

In spirit we are invited, yea, we are urgently commanded, to enter into the Holiest of All as purged worshipers. Where do you worship? If somebody were to ask you this question what would your answer be? Would you say, "In Moody Church?" That is a poor place in which to worship. How could you worship in the Moody Church, or any other church, *if the veil were not rent?*

Oh, dear Christian, do understand that they who worship the Father "must worship him in spirit and in truth." As we do this, where is the place of our worship? Not in any sanctuary made with hands, no matter how beautiful, how glorious, how grand, but only *inside the veil.* Your body may occupy a seat in some building, but if in spirit you come to God through the rent veil, the death of Jesus, and bow before Him in adoration, in love, in thanksgiving, in the name of His blessed Son, that is worship.

> "The veil is rent:—our souls draw near
>   Unto a throne of grace;
> The merits of the Lord appear,
>   They fill the holy place.
>
> "His precious blood has spoken there,
>   Before and on the throne;
> And His own wounds in heaven declare,
>   Th' atoning work is done.

" 'Tis finished! here our souls have rest,
  His work can never fail:
By Him, our Sacrifice and Priest,
  We pass within the veil.

"Within the Holiest of All,
  Cleansed by His precious blood,
Before the throne we prostrate fall,
  And worship Thee, O God!

"Boldly the heart and voice we raise,
  His blood, His name, our plea;
Assured our prayers and songs of praise
  Ascend, by Christ, to Thee."

True Worship

When people talk of worshiping in some building on earth, and think of a ritualistic service as worship, and talk of worshiping God in music, it simply shows that they do not understand what is involved in the rending of the veil. The worship that is acceptable to God is the music that rises up to Him as His Spirit touches the heart-strings of His redeemed people and we bow before Him, the Holiest of All, singing and making melody in our hearts unto the Lord. It is not merely that on Sunday mornings we press our way inside the veil; no, that is the place where we should be abiding in spirit constantly. Sometimes I go into a meeting where there is a very good atmosphere and some well-meaning brother rises to pray, and says, "O God, we thank Thee that this morning we have been sitting together in heavenly places in Christ." But it is not just when a good meeting is going on, but in every moment of the believer's life, he is sitting in heavenly places in Christ Jesus. The place of our abiding is inside the veil, in the immediate presence of God with nothing between. All that once shut God in and shut man out has been removed in the death of Christ.

Outside the Camp

But we must now consider the other expression, "Outside the camp," for what the old hymn says is true:

> "Our Lord is now rejected,
>   And by the world disowned;
> By the many still neglected,
>   And by the few enthroned."

Just as His place in glory is our place, so His place on earth is our place, as we go through this sinful world. What is His place down here? It is the place of rejection, for "He came unto his own, and his own received him not." These two expressions, "His own," are not absolutely the same in the original. The first is the neuter; the second is personal, and the passage may be rendered: "He came unto his own *things* and his own *people* received him not." Think of it, He came to His own city, Jerusalem, the city of the great King. If there was any place on earth where He might have expected to be received with gladness and acclaim, it was Jerusalem. He came unto His own temple, every whit of it uttered His glory, the very veil spoke of His perfect humanity, and every piece of furniture pictured Him. There was the altar, the laver, the candlestick, the table of shew bread, and everything spoke of Him; but as He came to His own things, the very priests in the temple joined in the cry, "Away with him, away with him, crucify him!" and they led Him outside the gate, the rejected One.

> "Our Man's rejected, don't you know,
> It happened many years ago,
> Yea, centuries have passed away
> Since it was great election day
> In Salem's city, e'en the same,
> Where God the Lord had set His Name."

There were two candidates that day, Christ and Barabbas. The people chose the murderer and rejected the Saviour.

He accepted the place they gave Him, and with lowly grace allowed them to lead Him outside the city, away from the temple, away from the palace, outside the gates, unto the place called Calvary,

> "And there, He died,
> A King crucified,
> To save a poor sinner like me."

As far as the world is concerned it has never reversed that judgment. He is still the rejected One, and the place the world has given Him should determine the place that you and I will take. He was rejected, not merely by the barbarian world, not merely by those who were living low, degraded lives, but also by the literary world, the cultured world, the religious world. It was the religious leaders of the people who demanded His death, and all the world acquiesced. The world still continues to do so. It has its culture, its refinements, its civilization (often mistaken for Christianity), its religion (one that has no place for the cross of Christ, or the vicarious atonement, or His glorious resurrection), but our blessed Lord is apart from it all, and the Word to us is this, "Let us go forth therefore unto him without the camp, bearing his reproach."

Sharing His Rejection

Do you rejoice in the salvation He purchased on the Cross, but shrink from participating in His rejection? Are you still seeking a place in the world that had no place for Him? Or, does your heart say, "We would not have joy where He had woe; be rich where He was poor"? Inside the veil —that is, the place of privilege; outside the camp—that is,

the place of responsibility. A beautiful little hymn puts it
this way:

> "Through Thy precious body broken
>   Inside the veil:
> O what words to sinners spoken
>   Inside the veil.
> Precious as the blood that bought us;
> Perfect as the love that sought us;
> Holy as the Lamb that brought us
>   Inside the veil.
>
> "When we see Thy love unshaken
>   Outside the camp;
> Scorned by man, by God forsaken,
>   Outside the camp.
> Thy loved Cross alone can charm us;
> Shame need now no more alarm us;
> Glad we follow, nought can harm us
>   Outside the camp.
>
> "Lamb of God, through Thee we enter
>   Inside the veil;
> Cleansed by Thee we boldly venture
>   Inside the veil.
> Not a stain; a new creation;
> Ours is such a full salvation;
> Low we bow in adoration
>   Inside the veil.
>
> "Unto Thee, the homeless stranger,
>   Outside the camp;
> Forth we hasten, fear no danger,
>   Outside the camp.
> Thy reproach, far richer treasure
>   Than all Egypt's boasted pleasure;
> Drawn by love that knows no measure
>   Outside the camp.

"Soon Thy saints shall all be gathered
  Inside the veil;
All at home, no more be scattered,
  Inside the veil.
Nought from Thee our hearts shall sever;
We shall see Thee, grieve Thee never;
'Praise the Lamb!' shall sound forever
  Inside the veil."

CHAPTER XII

PEACE BY CHRIST JESUS

"That in me ye may have peace" (John 16:33, R. V.).

HOW long it takes many of us to learn that peace is found in Christ alone. We seek for it everywhere else, but seek in vain, until at last, disappointed, disheartened and distressed in soul, we come to the Lord Jesus, and lo, at His feet our quest is ended!

Peace Better Than Happiness

Peace is far better than happiness. Happiness is primarily that which comes from a good "hap." "Hap" is an old English word for chance. Tennyson wrote of one "who grasps the skirts of happy chance." This expresses it exactly. If the "haps" are good, the worldling is happy; if evil "haps" befall him, he is unhappy. But peace is something deeper. It is the opposite of struggling, of warfare and of soul-unrest. It is freedom from strife, or from mental agitation. It is spiritual content such as the Lord promised to the heavy laden, when He said: "Come unto me. . . . and I will give you rest."

"O God," said Augustine, "Thou hast made us for Thyself, and our souls will never be at rest until they rest in Thee." And yet most of us spend years in restless seeking before we learn this lesson.

No Peace to the Wicked

This message is twice repeated in the book of Isaiah: "There is no peace, saith the Lord, unto the wicked." In chapters forty to forty-eight of this marvelous book, we have

118

Jehovah's controversy with idolatry. His people had sought in vain for peace, because they turned from Him, the true and living God, unto the senseless works of their own hands. Jehovah, the covenant-keeping God, stands in contrast to all the idols of the heathen. Therefore at the end of the forty-eighth chapter, there is this plain statement: "There is no peace, saith the Lord, unto the wicked." Then in chapters forty-nine to fifty-seven we have the great Messianic section of Isaiah, and we see the true Servant of Jehovah, the anointed Saviour, coming in lowly grace to His own, to open prison doors, to unstop deaf ears, to impart strength to feeble knees, and to give new life to those who are dead in trespasses and sins. But, also, we see Him spurned and rejected by those whom He loved so dearly, and in chapter fifty-seven, we hear the grave pronouncement: "There is no peace, saith my God, to the wicked."

How solemn all this is! No peace for the man who puts aught else in place of the Lord Jehovah in his heart and life! No peace for the self-willed rejector of God's blessed Son! In the New Testament, where we have the entire world brought in guilty before God, the solemn declaration concerning all who turn away from the Word of the Lord is this: "The way of peace have they not known."

A False Peace

There is also a false peace by which many are deceived. They mistake their ease of mind for peace of heart. Deluded by a false peace, and daubing their consciences with the untempered mortar of their own vain imaginings, they cry: "Peace, peace, when there is no peace." These are they who drift down the river of time, unaware of the awful precipice over which it will sweep them at last into the great sea of eternity, where they will be forever without peace and without hope. Of all such it is written: "When they shall say,

Peace and safety; then sudden destruction cometh upon them ... and they shall not escape" (1 Thessalonias 5:3).

If you try to awaken such from their deadly sleep and their false security, they are likely to turn on you with indignation. They do not want to be disturbed. Like the slothful man in the book of Proverbs, they cry: "Yet a little more slumber, a little more sleep; a little more folding of the hands in sleep." Alas, alas! If not awakened soon they will find out too late the folly of their assumed self-confidence.

One day, when walking along Broadway in Oakland, California, I saw ahead of me a man whom I knew was blind, making his way through the crowds with remarkable dexterity. He did not even have a stick, or a dog, to guide him. He had been over the same route so often that he felt sure he needed no help. Suddenly, I saw a cellarway opened just in front of him. In another moment he would have stepped down into the yawning mouth of a store basement. I sprang forward, caught him by the shoulder, and told him of his danger. Do you think he was angry with me for disturbing his false peace? Not at all! He thanked me profusely. But how different it often is with the unsaved man and woman. They go on heedless of their danger, and often resent the warnings of God's servants, until the Spirit of God awakens them to a realization of their true condition, and leads them to accept peace through the Lord Jesus Christ.

Two Aspects of Peace

In the fourteenth chapter of John, we learn that our blessed Lord, before He left this earth, said to His disciples: "Peace I leave with you, my peace I give unto you." Here we have two very distinct aspects of peace. One is that which He left as a settled thing when He went back to the Father's right hand, and is the result of His sacrificial work upon the cross, while the other is that which He imparts from day to day to those believers who live in fellowship with Him.

Sometimes people use expressions that will not always bear the test of Scripture. Let me give an instance of this: A number of years ago an earnest young Christian and I went to a mission in San Francisco. At the close of the meeting, a kind, motherly woman came to me, and asked: "Are you a Christian, sir?"

I replied immediately, "Yes, I am."

"Thank God," she said, and then turning to my friend, she asked: "And have you made your 'peace with God,' sir?"

Rather to my astonishment, he answered, "No, madam, I have not."

I knew he was a Christian, and I wondered at his replying in that way.

She said to him rather severely, "Well, if you don't make your 'peace with God,' you will be lost forever."

With a bright, happy smile on his face, he replied, "Madam, I can never make my 'peace with God,' and I never expect to try; but I am thankful that the Lord Jesus Christ has settled that for me, and through what He did for me I shall be in heaven for all eternity." He then put the question to her, "Have you never read that remarkable passage: 'Having made peace by the blood of his cross'?"

As he went on to explain it to her, the truth gripped my own soul. I saw then, and have realized it ever since, that sinners are saved through the "peace" which He made at the cross. And so we read in Romans 5:1, "Therefore being justified by faith, we have peace with God through our Lord Jesus Christ." This peace is not of our making, and is not of our keeping either. We enjoy the peace He made as we accept by faith the testimony of His Word.

His Peace is Given

But we also read, "My peace give I unto you." What does
the Lord Jesus mean by this? It is another aspect of peace
altogether. It is that quiet rest of soul which was ever His
in the midst of the most trying circumstances. He shares His
peace with us. It is of this we read in Philippians 4:6, 7:
"Be careful for nothing [or, In nothing be anxious, R. V.];
but in everything by prayer and supplication with thanksgiving let your requests be made known unto God. And the
peace of God, which passeth all understanding, shall keep
your hearts and minds through Christ Jesus." "The peace
of God," you see, is very different from "peace *with* God."
The latter has to do with the sin question, the former with
the trials of the way. It is the believer's privilege to bring
everything that troubles and distresses his soul to God in
prayer; to lay down every burden at the feet of the blessed
Lord, and to exchange them all for this wonderful "peace"
which is the portion of all who live in communion with Him.

> "Oh, the peace my Saviour gives,
>   Peace I never knew before;
> And the way has brighter grown,
>   Since I learned to trust Him more."